God Is Faithful

GOD IS Faithful

VELMA DARBO STEVENS

BROADMAN PRESS
Nashville, Tennessee

Library of Congress Cataloging-in-Publication Data

Stevens, Velma Darbo.
  God is faithful.

   1. Christian life—Baptist authors.   2. Trust in
God—Baptists.   I. Title.
BV4501.2.S7584   1986   231.7   86-921
ISBN 0-8054-5028-9

Contents

1.

God Is Faithful
(and Our Faith)

Faith in God through Jesus Christ is the most important doctrine of Christianity. We know that our salvation comes through this faith. We also affirm that all the other blessings of being Christians accrue through faith. (Note Rom. 1:17; 2 Cor. 5:7; Gal. 3:14,26-28; Eph. 6:16; 1 John 5:3-5—to name only a very few.) Perhaps, then, it is not surprising that most of our studies center around our own faith. We are told how necessary it is, and we are urged to act in faith. We are made to feel guilty when we don't "have enough faith."

I remember attending a faith-healing rally a number of years ago. The preachers warned the people that they had to have the "right kind of faith" for God to heal them. They must pray for "enough faith" for God to act. We people were even urged to buy some books that would instruct them in how to have a "healing faith."

Those preachers implied that God's healing power would work only in the presence of "healing faith." If the faith healer's touch or action did not heal, the fault would lie with the sick person! God was willing to heal. The faith healer was ready to pray for the healing to come. If it did

9

not, the X in the equation would be the sick person. There must be a hidden sin, a flaw, or a lack of faith.

But such teaching turns the whole matter of faith upside down. The important factor is not how much faith we have, but in whom we have faith.

Many people have abundant faith in the wrong things or in terrible people. Over nine hundred persons who died in Jonestown, Guiana, had plenty of faith in the Rev. Jim Jones. The problem was that he was totally untrustworthy. He led those people into the jungles to die—not to live.

So the theme of this book is the One who is totally faithful. This makes it possible for us to place our full trust in Him.

This, I believe, is the meaning behind Jesus' statement about faith as a grain of mustard seed:

"The apostles said to the Lord, 'Increase our faith!'

"He replied, 'If you have faith as small as a mustard seed, you can say to this mulberry tree, 'Be uprooted and planted in the sea,' and it will obey you" (Luke 17:5-6).

Jesus made it clear that the amount or the strength of faith was not at issue. God's power can and will work in the presence of even the smallest amount of faith. When God decides to move a mulberry tree at the request of one of His children, that mulberry tree is going to move!

Nothing is said about how God will do this or about how long it may take or what the result will be. All these matters lie within God's wisdom and in line with His purpose. Putting faith in Him includes allowing Him to make these decisions. This is why having faith in God is both safe and risky, both comforting and exciting. This is why having faith requires the trustfulness of the little child and the growing judgment of the maturing adult.

It is safe to trust God because He is utterly trustworthy,

but it is risky because we put ourselves totally in His hands when we trust in Him. We no longer can do "just what we want." God's faithfulness cannot be manipulated. He is not like the magic characters in fairy tales who are obligated to grant three wishes if a human being has the "secret word." This is why we must always pray, after asking for what we want, "Thy will be done" (Matt. 6:10, KJV).

It is comforting to trust God. He is the loving Heavenly Father. He will look after our welfare. But trusting Him is also exciting. He has made us partners with Him in the greatest enterprise in the universe. We are to work with Him in extending His kingdom until all human beings will acknowledge Him as absolute Ruler (Read 1 Cor. 15:24). Christ will bring all things under God's reign. Our task is to work under His direction to that end. This means that often our particular wishes may be denied or delayed. It is more significant to work for the Kingdom than to be comfortable, successful, or even happy! Our happiness, in the long run, does not come from getting our wishes. It comes from being part of the work of the Kingdom.

Further, trusting means to have the faith of the little child. The child does not ask how his/her parents work to bring about his/her welfare. The child does not question his parents' decisions. He trusts his parents' love, care, and wisdom. So it should be with us.

At the same time, God calls on us to share with Him as partners in the work of the Kingdom. This requires growing judgment. Throughout the New Testament, we are called on to *grow* (Eph. 4:14-16; Heb. 5:11-14; 2 Pet. 1:3-8). Part of growing is to exercise judgment and to learn to think first of God's work, not our own desires. Are you praying for the same kinds of things you did when you were first saved? Then you are still an infant in Christ.

Several years ago, I was working with a church group of college students. They were intellectually very smart. They attended a well-known university, and their college work included few "snap courses"! But when they talked about prayer, they complained that God did not answer them. They were praying for "things"—for their own desires to be given them. They wanted results at once.

I told them that they might be college students mentally, but spiritually they had not gotten out of kindergarten! When they cooled down from my statement, we began to talk about what it means to pray "in Jesus' name." Over the next few weeks, we all learned more about the way maturing Christians should pray.

So faith is the simplest element in the life of a human being. Anyone can exercise faith. But it also is the most demanding. The definition of faith found in Hebrews 11:1-6 may help to clarify these points.

The Nature of Faith
Hebrews 11:1-6

It would be a wonderful exercise to study the whole eleventh chapter of Hebrews in detail. Space does not permit this indulgence, so we will concentrate on the first six verses. Verse 1 gives a definition of faith. Verses 2-5 present examples of the working of faith in the lives of persons. Verse 6 shows how faith works.

"Now faith is being sure of what we hope for and certain of what we do not see" (v. 1). This is one major difference between faith and reason. Reason has to see, hear, feel, and otherwise use bodily senses to arrive at conclusions. Faith makes a leap beyond the senses. It does not ignore the circumstances in which it exists. But it

looks beyond, to where God rules. This is what Jesus and
His disciples did. They never lived in what we would call
"good conditions." But Jesus, and those who followed
Him, could speak glowingly of the future. That future, to
them, held glorious hope.

Hope and faith are intertwined and inseparable. If we
had no hope, we would have no reason for faith. Faith
gives certainty to our hope. We look beyond this life to
the glories of eternal life under the reign of God (1 Cor.
15:16-19). Faith says "amen" to our hope: it shall happen
because we believe God will be true to His promises.

Also, faith makes the unseen clear to us. No one has
ever seen God at anytime. Yet we believe in Him through
Jesus Christ. We do not have to trust our senses in the
spiritual realm. We trust in the One whom we cannot see.

"This is what the ancients were commended for" (v. 1).
They were not commended for their great works. They
are in our Bible because they were persons of faith. God
rewarded their faith by giving them a relationship with
Him. He still rewards our faith by giving us a relationship
with Him. So our faith has meaning for us now, as well
as in the hereafter.

Further, our faith deals with the past. "It is only by
faith that our minds accept as fact that the whole universe
was formed by God's command—that the world which
we can see has come into being through what is invisible"
(v. 3, Phillips). This statement beautifully interprets the
meaning of faith for the long-distant past. It makes "certain . . . what we do not see" (v. 1).

Scientists can deal with such questions about the universe as "How?" and "From what?" and "When?" But the
further they probe, the deeper grows the mystery of even
these questions. Every time scientists think they have
found the basic form of matter, others later uncover yet

smaller "building blocks." Every time scientists probe the far reaches of space with their telescopes, they discover even more worlds.

The principles of the origin of the universe, the laws by which it operates, and its ultimate fate are invisible. They are hidden in God's wisdom. God allows us to probe and to learn more all the time. But He moves even farther away from us, the more we probe. In the final analysis, only faith has the answer to the deep questions of our universe. These questions are: Who? and For what purpose? Faith answers: *God*, and, *so that He may have a universal kingdom of human beings who acknowledge His reign.* As we look into God's character and purpose, surely we will learn more about the answers to these questions. Thus your faith, for today as well as for the past and the future, will be more firmly fixed in him who is the faithful One.

Hebrews 11:4 speaks of the contrast between Cain and Abel. Notice that Abel's sacrifice was not better than Cain's just because he brought meat instead of grain. Abel made a better sacrifice because he acted out of faith. The inference is that Cain did not act out of faith. Perhaps he acted from duty or in order to make a better showing than his brother. Perhaps he did not care what the Lord wished in the way of sacrifice. One truth the story of Cain and Abel teaches us is that our works are never what save us. Only faith brings us into a right relationship with God.

This lesson is expanded in the story of Enoch (v. 5). He was victorious over death because "God had taken him away. For before he was taken, he was commended as one who pleased God." And how did he please God? In exactly the same way everyone can please God, as verse 6 tells us: "Without faith it is impossible to please God, because anyone who comes to him must believe that he exists and that he rewards those who earnestly seek him."

Of course the first step is to believe that God exists. Many people do believe this. Polls have shown that about 90 percent of Americans believe that God exists. It is the next step that marks the true believer—the faith that God will truly reward those who seek Him. It would be of little help to believe in a God who was not willing or able to help those who seek Him. Faith knows that God rewards. Faith also knows that God's rewards depend on Himself and His desires for persons. God rewards according to His will, not according to human will.

Therefore we need to know more about God: How do we know He is faithful? What assurances has He given us? What are His purposes, and how does He carry them out? What are the best rewards He can give His faithful people? When and how do they come? What will be the final reward for those who trust God?

These are the penetrating questions that form the structure of this book.

2.
God Is Faithful to His Name

How far can you trust God? This may seem like a very impertinent question. Surely we all can trust God to the limit—and beyond! But most people ask this question at some time or other in their lives. Some persons ask it all the time. Their answer is that one cannot really trust God. Others may not voice the question, but it comes out in their everyday living.

Many Christians have doubts about how far they can trust God with their day-by-day problems and decisions. They have trusted God with their past: they have trusted Him to save them through Jesus Christ and to cleanse them from their past sins. They have trusted Him with their ultimate future: they believe that when they die, they will go to heaven. But God seems remote from their present. They think of Him little as they go about their usual affairs. They may even believe that He is not concerned with such "ordinary" matters as how well they do their work, what kind of family life they have, or what decisions must be made in the course of a day.

Others trust God so long as everything is going well with them. They presume that success in work, good health, a happy family, and freedom from money worries are directly related to God's care for them. When some event occurs to shatter their serenity, their faith in God diminishes. They can trust Him totally only so long as He seems to be giving them all that they want from life.

A pastor talked with me about a deacon in his church. This man had been one of the most faithful members of the church; he and his family had attended regularly. He spoke often of God's goodness to him. Then his wife and daughter were killed in an automobile accident. He became bitter toward God, blaming God for these deaths just as he had praised God for the good things that had come his way. He no longer came to church, claiming he no longer believed in God.

There is a third type of belief in God which is closely related to the second. This kind of belief keeps demanding that God show His trustworthiness by granting personal requests. Such persons keep asking God for things important to them. They base their trust in God on His willingness to grant their requests. They never let themselves rest wholly on God's faithfulness because they never know when He might let them down!

All these kinds of belief in God fall far short of what God requires. He asks that persons trust Him for Who He is and for what He has promised to do. He does not play games with human beings, granting requests in order to show His faithfulness. This would become favoritism! Imagine Christians on two football teams, both sides praying for victory. God cannot, of course, grant victory to both. But if those praying are basing their faith in God on His answering such prayers, they are going to be disappointed.

But God does not ask for blind or ignorant faith. He has given all kinds of assurances to human beings that He will be true and faithful. The first requisite for faith on our part is a clearer understanding of God's faithfulness. The Bible is the record of God's faithful acts on behalf of humanity. This record is confirmed by the way God has worked in persons' lives through the centuries. It is also confirmed in our lives as we trust God for who He is.

God pledges to keep His promises by taking a solemn oath. He guarantees that His promises will be kept because of His nature. And He shows by His activities in history that He carries out what He has promised.

God Swears by Himself
Hebrews 6:13-18

When a new president of the United States takes the oath of office, he avows, "So help me God." When someone is asked to testify in court, that person is required to take an oath by God to tell the truth. When two persons make marriage vows, they do so "in the presence of God and these witnesses." They vow or swear by the highest they know: the Supreme Being, God. But when that Being wishes to take an oath, by whom or by what does He swear?

God swears by Himself. He is the greatest Being in the whole world. He has created the universe. Therefore, He is greater than anything in it or the sum of everything in it. If He swore by the earth or the solar system, He created all the elements of that system. He can destroy that system, then His oath could become null and void. Therefore, He swears by Himself. Isaiah 45:23 says: "By myself I have sworn." Hebrews 6:13: "Since there was no one greater for him to swear by, he swore by himself."

God goes even further in guaranteeing His promises. He swears by His name. To the Hebrew mind, a person's name revealed His character. People were sometimes given different names in order to show their changes in character. Jacob's name ("supplanter") was changed to Israel ("prince with God") to indicate his change in character. By what name does God swear?

His eternal name, which He revealed to Moses, is: "I am who I am." This name, given in Exodus 3:14, indicates one who is self-existent. No one can give Him a name. No one can characterize Him. No one can limit Him by time and space. He Who is always will be the same. Another translation of this name is, "I will be what I will be" (Note 14, NIV). No one can change God. He has absolute power over present, past, and future. For Him to swear by this name is an absolute guarantee that His promises will be kept.

Because God knows the tendency of human nature to doubt, He added guarantees to His promises. The best statement of this truth is found in Hebrews 6:13-18.

Abraham was the first person to whom God made His covenant promise. Genesis 12:1-3 records it. God told Abraham that if he would leave his land and migrate to a distant country, He would bless him greatly. He would make of Abraham's descendants a powerful nation. He would bless Abraham and in turn make him a blessing to all peoples. This was an unparalleled promise, where the God of the universe was willing to enter into an agreement with a mere human being.

It is not surprising that Abraham could hardly assimilate fully what God was promising. In fact, we see several times in Abraham's life where he retreated from his trust in God. He went down into Egypt during a famine instead of remaining in the land of promise (Gen. 12:10-20). At another time he tried to substitute Ishmael, the son of a slave woman, for the legitimate son God had promised him (Gen. 16; also Gen. 17:15-19).

At last came the climactic test when Abraham was ready to sacrifice his only son Isaac to the Lord (Gen. 22). God renewed His covenant with Abraham. But this time, He sealed it with an oath (Gen. 22:15-18). This is the oath referred to in Hebrews 6:13.

Notice that God swore by Himself "since there was no one greater for him to swear by." He was determined that Abraham should recognize how serious was His purpose. When God binds His promise by His oath, nothing can come between Him and the fulfilment of that promise.

Evidently this double guarantee—the oath and the promise—was enough for Abraham. Verse 15 states that Abraham was willing to wait to obtain the promise. This is one of the essential elements of faith: we must be willing to wait for God to act. The word translated "received" implies a bold acceptance of a promise whose fulfilment cannot be readily seen. This clearly describes Abraham's actions with regard to God's promise. He was willing to agree with God and to act as though the promise were being fulfilled, even when he could see no evidence of it.

The writer of Hebrews then applied God's action to all who have faith in Him—the "heirs of what was promised" (v. 17). He compared that action to contract disputes between persons (v. 16). In such disputes there is often a mediator or an arbitrator to help settle the questions. Then both sides sign a contract or take an oath that they will abide by the contract. The arbitrator works to see that both sides will guarantee their parts of the contract.

This is what God did, says the writer of Hebrews (v. 17). God acted as the arbitrator between Himself and Abraham. In that role, He exacted of Himself an oath to guarantee His promise. But He did not make Abraham take an oath!

What a generous concession for God to make! He has

no need to guarantee His promises—simply to state them. But He "wanted to make it very clear that he would never change his purpose" (v. 17, TEV). So He was willing to take the additional step of swearing an oath. Thus there are "two unchangeable things" about which God can never lie—the promise and the oath (v. 18). Because of them we have the strongest encouragement to put our trust in Him. He holds out to us the hope of His promises. We can "take hold of" that hope in the assurance that He will never fail us.

God's Nature Is Trustworthy
Exodus 33:18-23; 34:6-7

God's name expresses His nature. What is that nature? Swearing by Himself involves swearing by all that He is. This is another reason why we can trust God absolutely. He is not like the false gods of other religions: self-willed, selfish, aloof from the concerns of human beings, needing to be appeased by their worshipers. God is loving, righteous, dependable, trustworthy, powerful, wise, merciful, and yet able to be angry.

So God's eternal yes is based on his character. This is a never-changing character. We can continually learn more and more about it, but we will never understand all of it. Because God is infinite, He is unknowable in His total nature. The great joy for His people is the challenge to learn ever more about Him.

God always remains true to His character. Therefore, He remains true to His promises. He cannot cease to be Himself. If He makes promises based on His nature, He cannot and will not go back on them. To do so would be to deny His own nature. And if He did, He would cease to be the God of love, grace, light, power, wisdom, and holiness that He has revealed Himself to be. This is why

He will remain faithful to His promises, even when His people fail to keep their promises to Him (Read 2 Tim. 2:11-13).

Our passages from Exodus 33-34 are some of the best descriptions of the wonderful facets of God's character which can be found in the Bible.

God had become angry with the people of Israel in the wilderness. They had made a golden calf to worship, as they probably had seen done in Egypt. They had turned quickly from the worship of God alone. Only Moses' intercession kept God from destroying the people utterly (Ex. 32:7-14).

In the midst of this crisis Moses prayed that he might see God's "glory" (33:18). This is a difficult word. It appears many times in both the Old and the New Testaments. We use it frequently without having a clear idea of what it means. We know that it applies to God, but if someone were to ask us for an exact definition of "glory," most of us would find it hard to give.

But we find some clues in this passage from Exodus. God said that he would allow Moses insight into His "goodness" (33:19). But He would not let Moses see His "face" (v. 20). "For no one may see me and live." God thus equated "face" and "glory." God's "goodness" is seen in all His actions. But human eyes cannot stand the sight of His actual presence—His "glory."

The face is the human being's most perfect expression of personality. All of us have had the experience of seeing someone's back or walk and assuming that this person was someone familiar. But let the person turn to face us, and we see our mistake at once. The face clearly reveals the person.

So the "face" is the unique expression of God. It shakes the universe. It would be impossible to look full into the presence of God and live. It would be like looking full into the sun without going blind. We are warned, even during total eclipses of the sun, never to look at it without protective lenses. The rays of the sun are so powerful as to cause blindness even when they are obscured. This is a very feeble picture of the power and glory of God's presence.

So God would not expose Moses to a sight he could not bear. Instead, God promised His servant another view, which would satisfy his needs. Moses wanted to be assured that God's presence would accompany His people through the wilderness (33:14-16). So he asked to see God's glory. But God showed him a less dangerous view, yet one that equally assured Moses (vv. 21-22). God promised to show His servant His "back." This would be a reflection of His glory.

This has two probable meanings. One is that Moses was spared the full vision of God's presence while being assured of that presence. Another meaning is that God's presence is most generally seen after He has acted. God's "back" shows where He has been. Wherever God moves, God works. It is in God's actions that we really discover His nature.

What is that nature? Exodus 33:19; 34:6-7 tell us.

First God proclaimed His name, Yahweh (written as Lord, Ex. 33:19). This was the name revealed to Moses: "I am who I am" (Ex. 3:14). He has the power and right to act in any way toward His creatures. But His nature is such that He shows grace and mercy to all His creation without their deserving it. God always comes to us before we come to Him.

Exodus 34:6-7 expands this truth about God. These verses spell out the elements of God's nature. He is not only "compassionate and gracious," but he is "slow to anger." He can be angry, but He does not "fly off the handle." He abounds in "love and faithfulness." These elements are the inner core of His being. He shows this unchanging love to "thousands" by forgiving all kinds of "wickedness, rebellion and sin."

At the same time God does not let sinners get away with their transgressions. Those who persist in sin pass on these traits to future generations. The children learn about life from their parents and imitate them. And so the "sin of the fathers" is passed on to the "third and fourth generation"—unless the chain is broken when a member of that family repents and turns to the Lord.

GOD IS ALWAYS RELIABLE

The Bible shows us that God guarantees His promises on the basis of His oath, sworn by Himself, and on the basis of His total character. What other proof do we have that God really does keep His promises? All of human history points to that fact. It takes the eyes of faith to see God's workings. But to such eyes, His actions are clear. He always has been working. He has worked—and He does work—to carry out His purpose of salvation. These statements are faith statements. But they can be verified by looking at what God has done in history.

We will need to keep three points in mind, however, as we look. Otherwise, we may miss the true meaning of history. These points are:

(1) Don't judge God's activities merely by the way He acts toward individuals.

(2) Judge the present by the past; it often takes a long time to see the extent of God's activities.

(3) Remember that God acts in accordance with His total nature.

• Judge God's actions by history, not by acts toward individuals. No one has the wisdom to recognize all God's actions. We sometimes tend to think that God has answered our prayers when He may not have. For instance, when I was in college, I had the habit of staying late after classes to watch table tennis matches. Then I would run nearly all the seven blocks to the bus station to catch my bus home. All the way I would be praying that I wouldn't miss my bus. Most of the time, I didn't.

Looking back on these incidents, I do not believe that God was answering my prayers. For one thing, this late-afternoon bus was almost always late. I would manage to leave just in time to make it if it wasn't less than fifteen minutes late. Also, God's answering those prayers would have given me a wrong understanding of His actions. I deliberately made myself late. So I didn't have a good reason to beg God to make the bus late so I could catch it. I really did think, for a while, that this was what God was doing. It took some pretty hard lessons for me to learn that God doesn't deal with us like that. He will help us—but not to get us out of jams of our own making, except in rare instances.

On the other hand, we often do not recognize how God does answer our prayers. We may not get what we desire, but later on we see that God was working in our best interests.

There was a time in my life when I was seriously dating a man with whom I was deeply in love. To my great disappointment, he did not love me in the same way, and we broke up. For six months I mourned this loss. I had prayed earnestly that we would be married. He seemed to be just the kind of man I wanted to marry. Then one of my friends told me gently, but firmly, that he was glad this relationship had not ended in marriage. "You may think he's the same kind of person you are," the friend remarked. "But that really isn't so. He has very different values, especially in his religious life. I know you've been hurt, but I think this is the best for you."

Within a period of a few months, I began to see that this judgment was correct. God had answered my prayer. By telling me no, He had really said yes to my deepest desires —to have a marriage committed, on both sides, to God.

• Allow the past to interpret the present. This is always God's way of working. We cannot recognize God's providential working in history most of the time until after He has worked. Jesus' birth in Bethlehem had been foretold by the prophets. But the people of Israel were not expecting it. They had not understood the prophets' messages. Only in looking back at Jesus' life could the apostles relate the words of the prophets to the coming of God's Son.

As we look at the sweep of human history, we see truly that it is "His-story." God has been working out His plan of redemption through the ages, and we need to see that plan as it unfolded through the past.

The Israelites always looked back to the Exodus as evidence of God's working out His promises to Abraham and his descendants. We Christians look back at the cross and the empty tomb in the same manner. In Christ we see the greatest confirmation of God's promises to humankind (Read 2 Cor. 1:18-20). Every promise God has made to human beings finds its basic fulfilment in Jesus Christ. Because Jesus came, lived, died, and rose again to bring us salvation, we can trust God to keep all His promises forever.

• Remember that God will not violate His nature in carrying out His promises. God's actions over the sweep of history are true reflections of His total nature. Sometimes His acts of love are most clearly seen. At other

times, His judgment stands out. Consider His acts toward
Judah during the many years before they went into Exile
in Babylon.

For decades God continued to bless His chosen people
in spite of their sins against Him. At the same time, He
continued to send His prophets to warn the people: if they
did not repent of idol worship and of wrong dealings with
their fellow Israelites, they would be punished. But the
people looked only at what God was doing. They refused
to heed the warnings of the prophets. They interpreted
God's blessings as being unconditional. It did not matter
what they did, they thought. As the Chosen People, they
would always receive God's blessings.

Then came the awful judgment of bondage in Babylon.
Now it seemed that God had turned His face totally away
from His people. They could not believe that He would
ever bless them again. They felt that they were being
punished too severely. They failed to take into account
the sins of their fathers which they were repeating. The
rebellion against God was deeply ingrained. It would take
strong measures to root it out.

In both these instances, God's whole nature was being
satisfied. When He was blessing the people, His purpose
was to lead them to respond to His grace with faith and
obedience. When He punished the people, His purpose
was to lead them to turn to Him in repentance. Both His
blessing and His judgment were expressions of His stead-
fast love. He longed for His people to cling to Him in
obedience and love. But it takes a knowledge of history
to see these facets of God's nature working in harmony.

Sometimes God's acts of patience are misunderstood. It
may seem that God is indifferent or unseeing when He
does not act as soon as persons call on Him. But His
wisdom counsels patience.

Remember how long the children of Israel called upon God for deliverance from their mistreatment in Egypt. It seemed that God would never answer. But He was waiting for the right time. The children of Israel had to be so deep in misery that they would be ready to leave the country. It would require great courage for them to venture into the wilderness. Later, they had to carve out a homeland in a territory filled with hostile nations. In fact, more than once the Israelites were ready to go back to the slavery—and security—of Egypt. Only fresh memories of their enslaved condition and Moses' leadership kept them on course. If God had acted to deliver them as soon as they began to be persecuted, they probably never would have followed Moses out of Egypt.

All these three points reinforce the truth that God's actions must be judged by history. It is good for us to study biblical history. It is good, also, to study the history of Christianity. Over and over again, we see how God's providence has preserved His people through the centuries since Christ left the earth.

3.

God Is Faithful
in His Providence

Another sign of God's faithfulness is the way His providence works. We generally have a hazy, nebulous idea of what this word means. We tend of think of God's providence as unusual happenings or strange deliverances. "An act of God" is the way an insurance policy may describe a tornado, a flood, or a hailstorm: an occurrence that is far out of the ordinary. Therefore the insurance company will not be liable.

A person may speak of "God's providence" in being delivered from a natural catastrophe or in escaping from a terrible accident. A man who had survived such an accident with only cuts and bruises said, "I was scared to death the whole time. I was sure I was going to die. But Somebody was sitting next to me in that car! I don't know how else I escaped." But he did not stop to think that "Somebody" was sitting with him at all times. God does not limit His providential activity to times of special danger or extreme fear. The song goes, "My Lord is near me all the time."

Jesus had a clear understanding of God's providence. He asked, "Are not two sparrows sold for a penny? Yet not one of them will fall to the ground apart from the will of your Father. And even the very hairs of your head are all numbered. So don't be afraid; you are worth more than many sparrows" (Matt. 10:29-31).

Our problem probably lies, as it so often does, with our misunderstanding of the nature of God. We tend to judge Him by ourselves. And we tend to limit Him in the same ways that we are limited.

Haven't you heard people say, "Oh, God doesn't have time for my little problems"? Most of us have said this or at least thought it. But that is limiting God. We assume that He is bounded by space and time as we are. Yet God has all the time in the world—literally. He can be everywhere at once. He can concentrate on everything in the universe at one time. There is no way for our finite minds to comprehend these statements. We can only accept them by faith. Jesus did. But if we believe that God can be everywhere and in all time, we know that His care is active for every part of His universe at every moment.

Our second limitation on God is the way we compartmentalize His concern. We think of God as being more interested in the "spiritual" part of life than in the physical and mental well-being of His universe. Jesus attacked this idea in the words we have quoted. There is no part of His creation so insignificant that God does not pay full attention to it—whether it be a dying sparrow or the shedding of a hair.

If "providence" is not limited to special events or to special interests, what is it, really? The dictionary says that providence is exercising foresight, making provisions, or preparing. This definition refers to care, concern, and the ability to handle the problems of oneself or of others. It involves both the wisdom to understand the situation and the power to handle it. God has these qualities to the ultimate degree. Therefore, His providence is perfect, and it works for our benefit. Let us look at what is involved in God's power and wisdom.

God's Power and Wisdom
Isaiah 40:28

This verse stands within a great chapter of encouragement to the Exiles in Babylon. They had been surrounded for two generations by idols and idol worshipers. Many of the Jews had probably added these idols to their worship. Certainly God must have seemed to them unconcerned or else powerless, if He left them to suffer as captives in a strange land. The Babylonian gods must have seemed far more powerful! But the prophet Isaiah called them to remember the power of their own God. He could not be compared to any of these lifeless idols (Isa. 40:18-20). In fact He was and is the Creator of the world.

The *Lord*, in verse 28, stands for "Yahweh," the eternal name of God: "I am who I am." This uncreated God is the Creator of all things. "The ends of the earth" for the people of that day would have meant the farthest reaches which they could imagine. We might well expand the statement to say: "the ends of the universe." As our knowledge of the universe increases, our understanding of God's creative power should increase also. Whenever new worlds are discovered, they exist because God created them.

The last part of verse 28 speaks of God's power and wisdom. These are brief statements, but they carry a world of meaning for us.

God's Power.—"He will not grow tired or weary." Even the strongest beings we know—animal or human—do not have inexhaustible strength. Sooner or later they will grow weary. But God's power is as potent today as it was when He created the worlds. It will be as potent at the end of time as it is today.

Power has been defined as "the ability to accomplish purpose." Strength must be applied in such a way that a purpose is carried out. Power is meaningless unless it can be demonstrated through achieving a purpose. So God applies His power with His purposes in mind.

God's purposes relate to His love, mercy, wisdom, righteousness, justice, and holiness. They are consistent with His nature. Therefore, His power can be trusted. It will not be used in line with only one part of His character. God's power will not be applied simply to destroy, as an instrument of His wrath. Nor will it be applied simply to satisfy the desires of His children because He loves them. He will not make us "spoiled brats." God's power is always under the control of His will and at the call of His wisdom.

God's wisdom.—Isaiah 40:28 declares that God's wisdom is such that "no one can fathom" it. Isaiah 55:9 expands this idea: "As the heavens are higher than the earth,/so are my ways higher than your ways/and my thoughts than your thoughts." God's wisdom is far more than adequate for every problem or every question that may ever arise.

Wisdom is defined as "the power to see, and the inclination to choose, the best and highest goal, together with the surest means of attaining it." Consider what all these phrases mean with regard to God's wisdom.

"The power to see . . . the best and highest goal" means the ability to discriminate, to make the proper choices. Many persons seek goals. But it takes a truly wise person to understand which is the best goal to be sought. God's wisdom is perfect because He knows what the highest goals are.

Wisdom unerringly chooses "the best" goal. There is much difference between knowing the best goals and selecting them. This is a matter of will. God has the will to choose the best and highest goals.

Wisdom also involves the ability to determine the means of attaining its goals and the power to choose those means. This ability relates to judgment and intelligence. God has these attributes to the highest degree. Therefore, nothing can stand in the way of His achieving His highest goals.

Discrimination, will, judgment, and intelligence make up God's wisdom. This wisdom can be trusted. It will always work for the highest goals, and will direct God's power to the achieving of these goals. Thus God's power and wisdom combined guarantee that the highest welfare of His creatures will be unfailingly achieved.

God the Creator and Sustainer
Psalm 104

All of this psalm celebrates the power and wisdom of God. It portrays Him as the Creator of the world. It shows Him to be the Sustainer of everything He has made. Notice this general outline:

> vv. 1-4: God the Sovereign
> vv. 5-9: God the Creator
> vv. 10-23: God the Sustainer
> vv. 24-26: God the Creator
> vv. 27-30: God the Sustainer
> vv. 31-35: Praise of God

This is a magnificent psalm. It deserves reading and rereading. It would take too long to analyze the whole psalm. We will look at parts of it which emphasize God as Sovereign, Creator, and Sustainer of His world.

Read the psalm entirely. Study the particular verses analyzed here and see what is written about these attributes of God. Then read the entire psalm again. See how much more it means to you at the second reading.

God as Sovereign: vv. 1-4.—The picture here is of God's using the entire universe as His dwelling place. Certainly these verses do not mean that God is limited to a tent or a house, no matter how vast. All these statements about God are symbolic, not literal. The Hebrews often used concrete images to express spiritual truths. The truth here is that God is supreme over all His creation. He inhabits all space, as human beings inhabit their houses.

My husband and I have had the experience of moving from one house to another—a couple of times! With each move, we found the new house spacious and ready for us, but it seemed cold and unfeeling. As we moved in our furniture, hung pictures, and placed our prized possessions in strategic spots, the house itself changed. It became *our home,* expressing our character.

So God inhabits the universe. He does not need it, as we need houses, to live in. But by His presence, He stamps His character upon it. The first Soviet cosmonaut to orbit the earth declared that he did not find God in outer space. But he was speaking from the wrong perspective. He did not find God in his small, narrow layer of outer space because he had not looked for God on earth. To the eyes of faith, God's fingerprints are everywhere. He has stamped His character on His "home"—the universe—even as we stamp our personalities on our own homes.

God could not be the Creator and Sustainer of the universe if He were not sovereign. Otherwise, there would be a being higher than He. And that being would be the one who would ultimately decide the beginning and the end, the means and the purpose, of creation.

But God is absolutely sovereign. He knows no will but His own. He is before all things, the uncreated One. He is in control. His only limitations are those which He has placed on Himself in order to carry out His will. He is incomparable. There is no power, no being, in the universe that can stand before Him or against Him.

God as creator: vv. 5-9,24.—In poetic language, the psalmist traced God's creative activity from the foundation of the earth through the appearance of dry land (vv. 5-9). These verses proclaim the power of God and His absolute control over the world in the processes of creation.

Verse 24 refers to God's wisdom in creation. Think of the vast reaches of outer space where God's creative hand is revealed. Think of the infinitely tiny "inner spaces" where God also works. Compare the almost numberless kinds of life on this planet with the barren wastes of other planets in our solar system. God shows His wisdom in His ability to conceive of such a variety. Truly "the earth is full" of the creations of God.

Everything God has created expresses part of His character. The delicacy of a butterfly's wing and the bright colors of a hummingbird demonstrate His love of beauty in even the tiniest parts of His creation. The whale and the elephant, hurricanes and earthquakes, show His power. The cooperation of ants and bees, of wolf packs, and of nesting birds show something of the way God expects His creatures to live in harmony.

The worlds beyond worlds, seen in the farthest reaches of outer space that our telescopes can penetrate, move according to the laws which God laid down for them.

They do not deviate from these laws for even a second. So astronomers can predict the actions of heavenly bodies years in advance. If there are deviations, astronomers recognize that another element is involved.

An interesting illustration of this truth is the discovery of the planet Neptune in 1846. Astronomers had noticed a disturbance in the movement of the planet Uranus. This was the farthest distant planet then known. A French astronomer proved that this distrubance could come only from another heavenly body, but such a body was not yet located. The French scientist then figured out where such a body should be. Sure enough, other astronomers, working with his figures, found a new planet which they named Neptune.

Similar deductions, using God's unchanging laws of the universe, have led to the discovery of quasars, black holes, novas, white dwarfs, and red giants. So "The heavens are telling the glory of God;/and the firmament proclaims his handiwork" (Ps. 19:1, RSV).

There are also worlds within worlds. The atom is the smallest particle of matter which can exist alone. Yet it contains even smaller particles. The atom is mostly space, like the vast reaches of stellar space. There is a central core called the nucleus packed tightly with several kinds of particles. This might be compared to the sun in our solar system. Around the nucleus swirl numbers of particles called electrons. These may be compared to the planets orbiting the sun. How vast is the space in the atom? Imagine that the nucleus of an aluminum atom were the size of a marble. Then the outermost electron of that atom would be fifty yards away!

Thus God is the Creator of the very smallest as well as the very largest. Only infinite wisdom could conceive of such a world. Only unconquerable power could bring such a world into being. Furthermore, God did so out of nothing. Compare Genesis 1:2 and Hebrews 11:3.

God as sustainer: vv. 10-18,27-28.—The psalmist's praise of God's creative activity blends in these verses into praise of God as Sustainer. This is appropriate. God had to build into His creation the means of sustaining and continuing this life. Otherwise, His creation would have rapidly disappeared. In Genesis 1 we see that God created the elements of life—soil, water, light, and atmosphere (the firmament)—before He created plant and animal life. We see in this psalm the way God planned for His creatures to be sustained.

Running water and rain from above are needed for all kinds of life. Plants are necessary as food, directly or indirectly, for animals, fish, and insects. Think of how plant life sustains other life. Without it, all life would vanish from the earth.

A proper place to live is vital for the vast variety of created things. This is what we call "habitat." The habitat of a species is the area where it can obtain food and water, find a place to propagate itself, and have a reasonable degree of safety from the elements and its natural enemies.

This psalm rejoices over God's provision of habitats for His creatures. The birds have the trees for their nests, even the lofty cedars of Lebanon. The trees themselves have their own places to grow. The wild goats live in the rough, mountainous areas. The coneys (rabbits) find shelter among the rocks (vv. 16-18).

There are even proper times for these animals to come out and seek food. Some forage in the daytime, but others prefer darkness.

Habitat, food, water, shelter, and protection are necessary for God's creatures. It is fascinating to study how

God's providence cares for all His creation. Unless disturbed by humankind, birds and insects, fish and animals, grass and trees have their proper places to live. God's providence makes it possible for all these species to carry out His highest plan for them: to propagate themselves and thus continue to occupy their places in God's scheme of nature (Gen. 1:11,22).

Read this psalm again and see how beautifully all of God's creation fits together. Observe how each group has its own habitat.

Notice, too, how human beings fit into God's scheme of things. God's providence makes it possible for all of his creatures to be sustained and to continue on earth. He sets bounds and limits, so one part of His creation does not have to disappear in order for another part to survive.

GOD'S PROVIDENCE IN YOUR LIFE

When nature acts in its balance, the various parts of God's creation are sustained. Often human beings have upset this balance without providing other ways for God's creatures to be sustained. These actions by humankind are not part of God's plan for us to "have dominion" over all His creatures (Gen. 1:26). These selfish actions are born of our sinful nature, not of our being made in God's image. The picture of the Garden of Eden shows what God had in mind. Human beings were to tend God's creation and enhance it. They were to live in harmony with animals and plants, to "subdue" nature by increasing its beauty, usefulness, and harmony—not by destroying it.

Of course there are natural catastrophes which upset the balance of nature. Animals and plants may die in forest fires or lose their food supply in times of drought or flood. But taking the long look, we can see how God's sustaining work goes on. Individuals or groups may suffer or even perish. But the cycle of life is renewed each year in both plant and animal life.

What do these observations teach us about God's power and wisdom as these are exercised in our behalf? We are the highest of God's creation. Jesus kept urging His followers to believe that God would provide for all their needs (Matt. 6:25-33). He trusted His Father's power and wisdom. Can we do the same? Two major teachings come from our study of God's creative and sustaining work:

(1) God will always work for the highest welfare of His creation. In terms of lower species of life, this means their continual propagation and renewal. In the case of human beings, He defines this "highest welfare" in spiritual terms. He is most concerned with our spiritual life and growth. John 3:16 makes this clear. God's concern is our eternal spiritual life, not our fleeting physical life. In studying God's purpose in the next chapter, we will see more clearly what this "highest welfare" involves.

(2) God will work to keep the "balance" of care and concern for all persons. He will not help one person by hurting another. He will work with everyone who trusts Him until He can satisfy the needs and true desires of those involved.

These principles can teach us considerably about how we ought to pray. We need to make our desires and needs known to God, but we should not be inflexible about them. Instead of praying the same prayer over and over, we need to think of God's providential care for us and for all others. We should remember that God will not answer our prayers at the expense of others for whom He also cares.

During a hurricane season a group of Christians were praying that a particular hurricane would not strike near them and damage their equipment and buildings. They prayed for it to turn in another direction. Sure enough, the hurricane turned away from them. But it swung toward land again, rather than moving out to sea. It struck near a large city, and a number of people were killed.

Should we believe that God answered those Christians' prayers at the cost of other people's lives? In fact, should we pray for our own concerns without taking other people's needs into account? Part of praying for our own needs should include consideration of the needs of others. Thinking of them will broaden our vision of God's providence.

In 1980 most of the United States experienced a prolonged heat wave and drought. Here in Texas we had a record number of consecutive days with temperatures over 100 degrees. I prayed plenty about that problem. I prayed that God would break the heat and send rain. Then I read an analysis of the reason for this heat wave: a high pressure stalled over the Hawaiian Islands! It was not only bringing dry heat to the United States, it was also controlling the weather over Europe. They were experiencing unusually cold temperatures. I began to realize that "my" weather was much more than a local problem. It was global. By changing the weather in my area, who knew what might happen to the rest of the world?

Thereafter, I changed my prayers. I began to pray for the people who were suffering from the heat and drought. I prayed that aid would be given to those who had no air conditioning. I prayed that persons would have the wisdom to care for themselves. I prayed for the farmers, that they would be given financial aid to make it through the drought. My praying did not change the weather, but it changed my attitude and widened my concern for those in need.

Allow these two principles to work in your own praying. Make your requests known to God, but do not pray for one specific answer, and only that one, to be given. Leave room for God's providence to work in your behalf. Remember that He is concerned for your highest welfare. Ask Him to work in that direction in answering your prayer.

Also, consider the needs of others who may be involved in what you are praying for. Will this job for which I am asking mean that someone else will be put out of work? Does my prayer put me in competition with anyone else for certain favors? Ask God to use His providence to work with all who are involved in the situation.

Most of all, give God time to work. If He does not answer within your time frame, remember that He is working all the while. Read Psalm 37:4-7 and Psalm 40:1. Make these verses your motto. It is hard to pray with patience. But all of us learn through exercising patience every time we pray. And God is patient with our impatience!

4.

God Is Faithful
to His Purpose

God is faithful to His purpose. Of course, we are aware that God has a purpose for this world: It is to draw humankind to Himself and to bring to pass a universe where harmony, peace, love, and joy live eternally.

Christians acknowledge this purpose, but the final outcome seems far away. We recognize that Christ may return at any moment to bring God's kingdom on earth, but unfortunately that knowledge does not affect our everyday lives very much. We still act as if we will live forever on this earth. Or if the end should come, we feel that it will be by our death, not by the end of the world.

Feeling this way, we often find it hard to become excited about God's purpose or to live in conscious awareness of what He is doing in the world. In fact, some persons may use the fact of God's impending reign to excuse their not doing much about conditions here and now. One woman, discussing the problem of peace among nations, commented, "Peace will come only when we do it one on one." Then she immediately added, "Of course, that will only happen when Christ comes." She did not verbalize it, but her tone of voice implied that there was not much any of us could—or needed to—do about the problem of peace until Christ does return.

Another woman was defending inequalities among Christians of different races and social groups. A friend reminded her, "We are neither Jew nor Greek, slave nor free, male nor female, but we are all one in Christ Jesus." The woman looked astonished at having this verse (Gal. 3:28) quoted to her. "Oh, that happens only in heaven," she asserted.

Most of us, however, do not go even this far in our thinking about God's purpose and the end of time. We mostly live day to day. We think precious little of what effect our actions may have in this life, to mention nothing of their relationship to God's purpose.

Yet everyone longs to have a sense of meaning, a purpose in life. We want to feel that our lives have significance. Someone needs to care about us, to depend on us, to find life different because of us. For most people, these longings are fulfilled in their homes and families. Many persons find fulfillment in their careers. Some criminals even see significance in the evil they create. Political assassins often have this kind of motivation. John Hinckley, Jr., declared that he was "famous" because of his attempted assassination of President Reagan. Sara Jane Moore, who tried to kill President Ford, declared that she was "going to make a statement" by her act.

The problem with all these attempts at finding meaning in life is that they are only temporary. Families break up; children leave home; husbands and wives die or get divorced. I well remember my mother's saying, at the death of my father, "He was my whole life." They had had a stormy marriage, but it had lasted nearly fifty years. And my mother's whole purpose in life had been to care for my father.

Persons who have devoted their entire lives to their careers may be devastated by enforced retirement. I remember a couple who, childless, had poured their energies into their joint career. Six months after his retirement, he died of a massive heart attack. She went into a deep depression which lasted for several years. They seemingly had a powerful motive for living. When it was gone, there was nothing left—so far as they could see.

The reason for this human restlessness is found in our spiritual natures. We are not made for permanent residence on this earth. We long for significance beyond ourselves, beyond the limits of time and space. Partnership in the kingdom of God takes care of this longing.

The kingdom of God was the way Jesus described the working out of God's purpose in this world. The idea of "kingdom" is strange to us. The only "kingdoms" we know are the limited monarchies of Great Britain, the Netherlands, Norway, Monaco, and so on. But Jesus' hearers knew exactly what a kingdom was: we would describe it as a totalitarian government. The Caesars of Rome were absolute rulers. They owned everything and everybody in their territories. No law was higher than their will. No one had any rights that might conflict with the will of the ruler.

God also is absolute, but not in the same way. We saw in the last chapter that He is sovereign over His creation. No one has any rights before Him, but He does not rule by whim or in self-interest. His rule is for the good of all His creatures. Jesus indicated this by teaching that not even a sparrow would fall to the earth apart from the concern of the Heavenly Father.

Further, God has made plans for His world, plans which include human beings. He has chosen to make us partners with Him in bringing the kingdom of heaven on earth!

What greater significance could any person have than to share with God the Father, God the Son, and God the Holy Spirit the vast enterprise of making God's reign absolute on earth as it is in the rest of the universe!

God's Plan of the Ages
Ephesians 1:9-14

The entire letter to the Ephesians discusses the plan of God for His created order. At every point the letter shows what God is doing to bring His purpose to pass; and it shows how God's children fit into God's plan.

God did not keep this plan from humanity. Instead, "he made known to us the mystery of his will" (Eph. 1:9). The word *mystery* here does not mean an unrevealed secret, as it usually does to us. It had been unrevealed in past ages before the coming of Christ. Now it is an "open secret," to be declared to the whole world. But Paul did not mean that nothing was known of God's plan during Old Testament days. Many times in the Bible, God's plan is referred to. But often those who read or heard of God's plan did not understand it. Only with the revelation of Jesus Christ was the "mystery" made plain.

As we study the entire Bible, we can see how God's plan unfolded. It began "before the creation of the world" (Eph. 1:4). God created a universe of order, harmony, power, and beauty through which to express His glory. The word *glory* means, among other things, the expression of God's character and personality (recall the study of Ex. 34:6-7 in chap. 2).

As we saw in the last chapter, God's character is impressed on His creation, but God wanted to do more than this. He wanted to have creatures made in His image to have fellowship with Him. Because they were like Him in nature, He intended for them to grow more and more like Him; and He desired for them to rejoice with Him over the wonders of His creation.

God's desire for such fellowship led Him to take a risky step. All other parts of His creation obeyed Him because they could not do otherwise. Wind and lightning, planets and comets, atoms and living things obey God's laws from necessity. But God did not want His highest creatures— humankind—to behave in this way. Because God is love, He wanted human beings to love Him *freely*. He desired that they come to Him in love in response to His offer of love to them.

To make this possible, He created human beings with free will. They were thus able to answer either yes or no to His offer of love and fellowship. He knew, of course, that many, many would say no. But He also knew that many would say yes. For the sake of these and the fellowship they would enjoy with Him—and He with them— He set up a situation where humanity could defy Him.

And human beings did! They used their free will, not to respond to God, but to rebel against Him. But they could not overthrow God's plan. He had made provision for this result in the very act of creating. He already knew the steps He would take—clear through the cross—to reconcile His rebellious creatures to Himself. He would do this through revealing Himself as Holy Love and calling for a response of faith and obedience.

Both holiness and love were needed to call forth the response which He desired. If God offered only His love, persons might feel that they had no obligation to live according to any moral standards. If God acted only according to His holiness, human beings would be absolutely unable to meet His standards. God's plan was that both His holiness and His love would be satisfied. Repentance and confession—offered to God, believing that He would forgive sins—satisfied God's holiness. Love and obedience, offered in faith that God would receive these, satisfied His desire for fellowship. These themes will be expanded in chapters 5—6.

This was God's plan. But it took several thousand years for it to come to maturity. Meanwhile, God was working to reveal Himself to humanity. He could have done this directly. Instead, He worked through persons who responded to Him in faith. It was His plan that those who related to Him in faith, love, and obedience should show Him to others. Then they, too, had the option of responding to God in faith.

God carried out this part of His plan through His covenant relationship with individuals, groups, and nations. We will study this in detail in chapter 7. In the meantime, consider three responses which God demanded from those who would be His people:

(1) Recognition of Him as Supreme Being, to whom total allegiance was owed (Deut. 6:4-5)

(2) Faith that He would fulfil His promises to His people (Deut. 6:10-12)

(3) Obedience to His will as shown in His moral demands (Deut. 6:18-19,24-25)

All these requirements are intertwined. Each depends on the others. Keeping one involves keeping all three. Those persons and groups who responded to God in these ways would not only be acceptable to Him, but they would reveal Him to the unbelieving world. This was the purpose of God's covenant relationship: to be for "the praise of his glory" (Eph. 1:12-14). As more and more people saw God's "glory"—the knowledge of His redeeming character and His holy love—they would be led to make similar responses to Him.

At last, "when the time had fully come, God sent his Son" (Gal. 4:4). This was the final step which He had envisioned from the beginning of His plan. Jesus Christ would complete the revelation of God and the work of reconciliation. (These steps will be more clearly shown in the chapters on holiness, love, and the final triumph of God.)

Because Jesus so perfectly revealed God, and is God, the Father has put the whole universe under the reign of Christ (Eph. 1:10). God's original purpose was to have a universe of peace, harmony, and order. Such harmony requires one head, one rule of authority. God has appointed Jesus Christ to be that head. Under His rule there will be no alien elements, no discordant notes, no rebellion against God. Also, Jesus will unite all the elements of creation. They will find in Him what cements them together.

This is appropriate. Jesus is the God-man. He unites in Himself all the elements of the divine and the human. He is the Word by which the world was originally created (John 1:3). He is also the power by which the world will be re-created (Col. 1:15-20).

This climax and completion of God's plan will be "put into effect when the times will have reached their fulfillment" (Eph. 1:10). Even Jesus did not know when this would happen (Matt. 24:36). So it is not our business to try to figure out when the "times" will be fulfilled. Our business, as Jesus repeatedly told His disciples, is to be faithful (Matt. 24:42-47).

The major part of God's plan, however, involves what He is doing and will do with those who respond to Him in faith. We have "been predestined according to the plan of him who works out everything in conformity with the purpose of his will" (Eph. 1:11). Earlier Paul said, "In love he predestined us to be adopted as his sons through Jesus Christ" (v. 5). Don't let that word *predestined* throw you. It simply means that God planned to have children who would be "adopted" through Jesus Christ. It would be like saying that human couples "predestine" the rearing of children. If they have children, their plan is to rear them to maturity. Human parents cannot guarantee their plans. But God guarantees His purposes. What He plans, He can and will carry out.

This idea of adoption is fascinating. In Roman law a natural child could be disinherited, driven away from home, or even killed. But if a man adopted a child, he could never disinherit him. The force of Roman law stood between the man and his adopted son. If the law stated that this was the man's son, he had to continue to acknowledge the boy. This is how God has chosen to relate to us.

The purpose for which God "predestined" human beings to be His children is for "the praise of his glory" (Eph. 1:12-14). Through the genetics of human birth, children bear the physical, emotional, and mental characteristics of their parents, at least to some degree. We often speak of a "family likeness." So human beings, born again through the power of the Holy Spirit, are to bear the likeness of their Father.

Jesus said, "Anyone who has seen me has seen the Father" (John 14:9). All who have been born by the Spirit bear a likeness to Jesus Christ, which needs to increase daily as we grow in grace (Eph. 4:13). So all Christians show forth the "glory" of God. We express in our own selves the love, righteousness, holiness, compassion, hatred of sin, and other characteristics that make up the character of God. We do this very feebly, of course, but God has entrusted His "glory" to us. We carry on the work of Jesus Christ in the world—the work of revealing the Father.

Thus God's purpose has never changed. He has continued to use persons of faith to reveal Him to the world. At the end He promises rich rewards to his children: an "inheritance . . . the redemption of those who are God's possession" (Eph. 1:14). We bear God's image in a muddy, indistinct manner now, but the day will come when we shall fully reflect Jesus Christ. Then we will reveal our likeness to God as a cloudless sky reveals the brightness of the sun. "Then the righteous will shine like the sun in the kingdom of their Father" (Matt. 13:43).

Humanity's Part in God's Plan
Romans 8:15-17

The passage in Ephesians gives the broad outlines of God's plan. These verses from Romans 8 fill in much of the outline which deals with humanity's relation to God's plan.

Verse 15 points to the new condition of those who have accepted Christ as Savior. We have a new spirit, a new nature. Before coming to Christ, we—like all human beings—were in slavery to sin (Rom. 6:11-14). Paul continued in that chapter to use the figure of slavery. Christians have exchanged masters—from evil to God (Rom. 6:15-18). They owe absolute obedience to God, as slaves owed total allegiance to their masters.

In Romans 8 the figure is changed. Now the relationship with God is one of child and parent. So our spirit is not one of fear. Our relationship with God is based on love. This relationship is characterized in three ways.

(1) The spirit we now have is not one of slavery but one of "sonship" (v. 15). This is the same word translated "adopted" in Ephesians 1:5. It carries the same meaning of an unchangeable relation between child and father.

(2) This sense of relationship is warmed by the way we can respond to our Father. This is not merely a formal child-parent relationship. The word *abba* is Aramaic for "father" (v. 15). The family language of most Jews was Aramaic. So a little child would learn to call his father "Abba," as we learn to call our fathers "Daddy" or "Papa." So our relationship with God the Heavenly Father is the loving relationship of a small child with his parent.

Nor do we have to rely on our impulses to be sure of this relationship. The Holy Spirit Himself assures us inwardly that we are children of God. What we know by faith is borne out by experience. Living day by day under the Spirit's guidance, we gain more and more assurance of God the Father's love toward us.

(3) We are not only children of God—but heirs. Inheritance was especially important in biblical times. Nearly all wealth was in real property—land, cattle, precious metals, and so on. The sons of wealthy parents were dependent on them until their time came to inherit. Without such an inheritance, a child could quickly become destitute (compare the parable of the prodigal son).

Romans 8:17 asserts that we are more than heirs. We are "co-heirs [or "joint heirs"] with Christ." This means we shall totally share in what comes to Him from the Heavenly Father. This is described as "glory." This word, as we saw in chapter 2, relates to the expression of one's character in ways that can be observed. Christ's glory is the shining forth of His wonderful character. We will share in this glory.

But such a wonderful result is not gained without a price. For the Christian, that price is to "share in his sufferings" (v. 17). Christ suffered in the flesh in His contacts with the sin and evil of the world. So Christians will suffer as they stand before and against evil. Living as God's child in the world means to live as He does, in conflict with evil. This conflict elicits suffering. But it is creative suffering because it works for good.

Partners in the Kingdom
Matthew 5:13-16; 25:19-23

Notice to whom Jesus spoke these words. These were "His disciples" (Matt. 5:1). Yet, there is no indication that only The Twelve were included. Read Matthew 7:28: "The crowds" listened to Him. They were not a small group of ordained or dedicated persons. They were the large mass of Jesus' followers. Jesus called these ordinary people "the salt of the earth" and "light of the world" (vv. 13-14). Both of these elements are pivotal in the lives of human beings.

Salt is both a preservative and a flavoring agent. It was much used to preserve food in the days before canning and freezing were possible. So Jesus taught that his disciples would help to preserve what is good in the world through their presence.

Light is the means of illumination. Without it, life would not be possible. Jesus was speaking here of the lights which persons use in the darkness—lamps. With no light to drive away the darkness, persons would be doomed to active life in the daylight hours only. The lamps of Jesus' day were poor means of illumination. Today a whole range of life is open to us because of our electric lights. Jesus emphasized that His disciples brought light into darkness, making it possible for human beings to live and showing them what is real. In the darkness, all things seem alike. It requires light to reveal truth.

God could have, all by Himself, sent "salt" and "light" into human lives. But He chose to use His redeemed children for this task. Notice several facts about Christians as salt and light.

Salt works quietly and secretly. Its presence is best known by its effect. Light is seen but does not call attention to itself. Rather, it shines so what is important can be seen. Both these elements work according to what is natural to them. Also, Jesus did not teach that individuals must work alone in being salt and light. He addressed His words to His disciples as a group. One grain of salt can do little. One small lamp cannot shed much light. But put together, these grains and these lamps can have a powerful effect on their environment.

God intends for His children to work like this in the world. Sometimes their presence will be noticed; sometimes, hidden. Yet, the effect will be to present wholesomeness and revelation to the world.

This effect is summed up in verse 16: Jesus said that we are to shine before men. We are to reveal God through our lives and our words, our attitudes and our actions. Then others will see in us, not ourselves, but our Father, who is the author of everything good we do. The result will be to give praise to the Heavenly Father. This praise will turn sinners to God, reveal His goodness, and show persons how to live in righteousness.

But there is more to the partnership than this. God is preparing us for greater service and more responsibility in His kingdom in eternity. This is an emphasis which is not often made. But Jesus' words clearly reflect the fact. He talked with His disciples about their future power and places of responsibility (Matt. 20:20-28; 19:28). Some of His parables, presented right before His death, also have this emphasis. Look at Matthew 25:19-23.

This is the familiar parable of the talents, in fact, one of a series of parables which Jesus gave at the end of His life here. He had turned His attention away from the unbelieving Jews and toward His disciples. As He prepared them for His departure, His theme was faithfulness and its reward.

You remember that in this parable of the talents, the man who had earned five more talents was awarded the talent which had been entrusted to the unprofitable servant. I used to struggle over this part of the parable. It seemed unfair that the man with the most talents received another one. But the clue comes in verse 21: "His master replied, 'Well done, good and faithful servant! You have been faithful with a few things; I will put you in charge of many things. Come and share your master's happiness!' "

Often, in thinking of this parable, we pass over the new responsibilities assigned to the faithful servants. We think only of entering into the "joy" of the master. But these men were servants entrusted with their master's property. Their job was to increase his wealth, according to his command. The highest reward to them would be to receive more responsibility—a promotion, we would call it. Faithful workers in a business corporation do not dream of being allowed to sit down and be lazy. They dream of becoming a vice-president!

So the point of Jesus' parable to His disciples was this: Do faithfully what you have been called to do. Use your life, your abilities, and your energies to advance the kingdom. Then you will be fitted for bigger responsibilities in the full reign of God's kingdom.

Sometimes we hear Revelation 14:13 quoted to bolster the idea of there being no work in heaven: "They will rest from their labor, for their deeds will follow them." But this is a different kind of "labor" from the creative work of God's kingdom. Dr. Ray Summers, in his commentary on Revelation, explains the verse:

> The word for rest, . . . literally means "they shall be refreshed." The word for labors, . . . literally means "toil under great adversity." They are thus refreshed after great toil. . . . The Christian . . . makes an abundant entrance with all his genuine works for the Lord. He does not go empty-handed as a one-talent servant but as one who has used every opportunity to invest himself profitably for the Lord.[1]

Those who have "toiled" on earth will be refreshed. And they will be given opportunities—of which we cannot dream now—to further use their talents in the widest stretches of God's kingdom. (We will see more about this in the final chapter of this book.)

YOUR PLACE IN GOD'S PLAN

At the beginning of this chapter, it was stated that every person longs to have meaning in life. No meaning could be more significant than to have a share in God's purpose of bringing His creation to fulfilment.

God's plan throughout the ages has been to use persons who are faithful to Him as the means of completing His purpose. This means every person who has accepted Christ as Savior has been reborn into His likeness. This responsibility is not something that can be accepted or rejected. It belongs to every Christian by birthright. The only choice is how well each person will carry out this responsibility.

Parents used to tell their children it was their job to "carry on the family tradition." This meant that the children were to enhance the family honor and to teach their own children what it meant to come from that special family. This is a small picture of our responsibility as children of the Heavenly Father. We bear His name and His likeness through faith in Jesus Christ. What we do with that name will further His kingdom or retard it. We can "shine" in our daily living, so people will be more inclined to turn to Jesus. Or we can hide our light, so people will still stumble in darkness.

Living as children of God is a "natural" (or supernatural) response for redeemed persons. It is not something alien. We have to struggle with our human nature which is so familiar to us. But whenever we act in line with God's purposes, there is a sense of rightness and fitness in what we do. We feel "at home" in obeying God.

How do you know when you are acting as a partner in God's kingdom?

First is the question of relationship to Him. Is Jesus Christ your Savior? Have you accepted what He has done for you in order that you may be a part of His kingdom and a child in His family?

Do you also recognize Jesus Christ as the absolute Lord of your life? It is unfortunate that these two emphases— Savior and Lord—have been separated in evangelistic witnessing and preaching. There is no way for Christ truly to be your Savior if He is not Lord of your life. That is the witness of the whole New Testament, but God is patient with our failures to understand. He has put His nature within us, and this nature desires to do His will.

So Jesus is the Lord of our redeemed personalities. Our need is to devote our wills and our efforts to knowing and doing the will of God. This ancient prayer, simply phrased, could be the prayer of every Christian:

> Day by day,
> Dear Lord, of Thee three things I pray:
> To see Thee more clearly,
> Love Thee more dearly,
> Follow Thee more nearly,
> Day by day.
>
> —Richard of Chichester

We can do this by considering again the three responses God requires to His revelation of Himself:

(1) Recognize God as Supreme Being, to whom total allegiance is owed.

(2) Believe that God will fulfill His promises to His people.

(3) Obey God's will as shown in His moral demands.

Ask yourself how well you are carrying out these responses in your life. Where does your loyalty to earthly concerns and interests keep you from giving total allegiance to God? My father was a naturalized citizen of the United States. He still loved the "old country"—Norway —from which he came. But he was fiercely loyal to the land to which he had pledged allegiance. Becoming a naturalized citizen involves renouncing all allegiance to the person's former nation. My father firmly believed this.

How much do you need to grow in your belief in God's promises? This is a question that will continue to be asked as this book progresses. Is your faith the childish kind that demands God's giving in to your every whim and desire? Where this is true, you need to grow in understanding His promises and how He fulfills them in human lives.

Are you sincerely seeking to do God's will in your everyday life? Often we think more about "finding" God's will than about "doing" it. *If I just knew God's will, I would do it,* we often say or think.

A pastor preaching a revival in our church expressed it well: "We need not concern ourselves about 'finding' God's will. There is more information about God's will in the Bible than we ever carry out. If I were to hang a banner with one statement of God's will on every line of the wall of this church, the whole building would be covered."

Consider all the statements of God's will that you already know. Devote yourself to carrying out these expressions of His will as best you know how. As you do that, you will continually learn more about His will.

Being a partner with God in His kingdom enterprise means responding in the three ways stated above. When we do, we continue His revelation of Himself to the world. And doing that brings His kingdom—His rule in the hearts of men—even closer. For those who see our "good deeds" will give "praise" to the Father and also acknowledge Him as their Lord through Jesus Christ.

NOTE

1. Ray Summers, *Worthy Is the Lamb* (Nashville: Broadman Press, 1951), p. 182.

5.
God Is Faithful in His Love

We have seen that God's purpose is to win the world of humanity through revealing Himself as Holy Love: "God is love" (1 John 4:16). This statement has been familiar to many of us from early childhood. This is the capstone of God's character. It is the central element of His nature around which all the other elements revolve. It should be the easiest of all His character traits for us to understand and lay hold on.

But it is not so easy as we may think. Our ideas of God's love may be shaped by the human love—or lack of it—which we have experienced. We accumulate certain ideas about God's love (perhaps as children) which are hard to erase. And no one, however mature, ever fully understands the nature and the power of God's love. There is always more to learn. Consider some of the distorted ideas of God's love which various people have.

Some people see God as a stern Judge, not as a loving Heavenly Father. A young man declared that he could not relate to God. He saw the Father in terms of his own earthly father, a stern and judgmental man. That father demanded perfection from his son. Every lapse was treat-

ed with harsh discipline. This young man confessed that
he could believe Jesus loved him—but not God. He could
not identify Jesus with God.

Some people, on the other hand, see God as an indul-
gent "Daddy." They live as if God existed to meet their
every need. They constantly pray to him for everything
they desire. They are offended if they do not receive the
answers to their prayers immediately—and exactly as
they requested.

Some people act as though they were playing games
with God. They pray with the idea that if they do something "right"—have more faith, listen to the right preacher, give to a certain cause, and so on—God will
immediately answer their prayers. I heard one television
evangelist tell his audience that if they would lay their
hands on their television sets, God would immediately
heal their ailments. In such circumstances, nothing of
seeking God's will or desiring His will to be done seems
to enter the picture.

Other people act as though God's love is the door to
heaven, and that is all that matters. If their names are
"written in the Lamb's book of life" (Rev. 21:27), they
reason, they are set for eternity. God's love is simply the
means of escaping hell and (often secondarily) gaining
heaven.

Some persons view God's love as mere sentiment. They
think of having fellowship with Him as an exercise in
sharing feelings. They sing, "Oh, How I Love Jesus,"
without considering what they should do about this love.
If someone were to tell them that loving Jesus means
obeying His commandments, they might be astonished.

Some people go on taking God's love and care for granted until some tragedy befalls them. Then they feel as if
God has betrayed them. The "normal" state of affairs,

they think, should be never to have sickness, trouble, or death. When trouble comes, they believe that God has turned against them. They asked, "Why me?" not "Why not me?" They do not understand the biblical statement, "Man is born to trouble as surely as sparks fly upward" (Job 5:7).

Others believe that God must "prove" His love for them in extraordinary acts. *If God loves me,* someone reasons, *He will see to it that I get my prayers answered in some miraculous way.*

I fell victim to this kind of thinking about God when I was in college. I was a "Christian service volunteer," and my parents were poor. I was in college on a scholarship, but I had to pay certain expenses myself. The college had a rule that all bills must be paid before students could take semester exams. Otherwise, they were barred from the exams, and they would fail all their courses.

At the end of the first semester of my senior year, I needed two hundred dollars to complete my payment. I had been reading a lot of Christian biographies such as George Mueller, J. Hudson Taylor, and "faith missionaries." My imagination was inflamed by my reading. I decided to trust God in the same fashion as some of these persons did. They had not let anyone except God know of their material needs. And lo and behold! Those needs were met in strange and mysterious ways.

I decided to do the same. I could have written to my father for the money, and I knew that he would have raised it somehow, but I decided to trust God to raise up an unknown benefactor to send me the two hundred dollars. I felt that this would be a sign of God's favor on my decision to work for Him in a full-time religious profession.

For the next couple of weeks I watched the mails, hoping to find my money. I was in an ecstasy of anticipation, wondering who my "unknown benefactor" might be. But nothing came.

By the morning of my first exam, I was almost in a panic. If no money came, I could not take my exams. If I did not take them, I would fail my courses. I could not graduate in May.

There were two mail deliveries before exam time. Nothing in the first mail! But in the second was a letter from my father. He enclosed a check for two hundred dollars, saying that perhaps I might need it.

I was both relieved and humiliated. I was humiliated to think that I could have obtained this money simply by writing my father. Maybe I hadn't needed to do all that praying after all! It was as if God had answered both yes and no to my request for a "sign." He had motivated my father to send me the money. But perhaps He had not done anything "miraculous" for me.

I meditated on this occurrence for quite a long time. My humiliation turned to humility. I realized that God had shown me His favor by teaching me a valuable lesson: I could pray for what I needed, but I must not presume to dictate to God the means or the timing of His answer. The "how," "when," and "where" of His answers belong to Him alone.

Most of you have probably experienced some of these "tainted" ideas about God's love at various times, as I did. We may entertain other ideas that similarly misunderstand the nature of God's love.

It is essential to see that God's love is an expression of His total nature. All the qualities of His character are seen in His love, and His love is influenced by these qualities. God's love has been seen throughout human history: in His creative love, in His seeking love, in His redeeming love, and in His triumphant love. These truths about God's love are taught throughout the Bible. But they are distilled in their purest essence in the verse which we call the "condensed" Gospel—John 3:16.

The Sweep of God's Love
John 3:16

God's creative love.—"God so loved the world."

This shows the motivation of God in creating His universe. In the books written by John, the word *world* has two different meanings. In one sense "world" means the rule of evil on our planet. Jesus used the word in this sense when he said, "If the world hates you, keep in mind that it hated me first" (John 15:18). The other use of "world" is to mean all of God's creation. It is used like that in John 3:16. (Both meanings of the word are seen in John 1:9-10.)

In creating His world, God made provision for creatures who would be like Him and who could have fellowship with Him. He gave them free will, so they would respond to Him freely in love.

He created a beautiful world for them. It is true that there are both unpleasant and terrible things in this world —rattlesnakes and typhoons, earthquakes and pestilence. But outweighing these are the daily proofs of God's providence. The sun rises and sets. Rains fall. Plants grow. There are families to care for children. People have mental and physical strength to make a living. Human beings live in a social world where they can cooperate in joy and service. Most important is that God's presence and power are available to those who will love and trust Him. The theme of the universe was planned to be joy: human beings rejoicing in God's love and God rejoicing in how persons respond in love to Him.

As we know, things did not work out as planned. Human beings used their free will to rebel against God, not to obey Him. They did not trust His creative love for them. They believed that obedience to God would have been slavery, whereas it would have been true freedom. When God creates, His love leads Him to make possible the highest achievement of His purpose.

All human beings are created "special." Each person is unique, with special abilities, personality traits, and potentials. This is part of what it means to be made "in the image of God." So God's creative love broods over His creatures. Obeying Him would mean not losing our personalities but finding them. In becoming like Him, we become our true selves. This happens from at least two standpoints.

One is through fellowship with Him. We become like those whom we love. Some friends of mine adopted a baby girl. She was like them in coloring but not in features. One day, when she was about six months old and had been with my friends for several months, I looked at her and thought, *Why, she really does look like _____ after all!* Her features were still the same, but her smile was her adoptive mother's. She was growing like her by living in the light of her love.

A second way to become our true selves is to obey God's will for us. Again we can observe how earthly parents act. Sometimes parents are wise enough to train their children in the direction of their true abilities. Let us say that parents observe their son continually playing with musical instruments. If they are wise, they will give such a child music lessons. If a girl shows mathematical ability, she may need to be guided toward accounting or computer science.

God is always nudging us toward the fulfillment of our

profoundest abilities. Obeying Him means to fulfill our potential.

I determined to make religious service my career. Before that, my obsessive ambition had been to write. When I turned to a church-related career, I tossed my writing ambitions out the window. I had never heard of writing as a religious career, so I assumed that it had no part in my future.

Less than ten years later, I learned of opportunities in religious journalism. For the first time, I realized that I could combine my talent and my desire to serve God. Joyfully, I entered upon a career in religious journalism. God has blessed me with growing effectiveness in this area. He knew, better than I, where my real talents lay. Obeying Him led me to fulfill my potential.

God's seeking love.—"God so loved the world that he gave his one and only Son."

What happened when God's original plan did not work? Was He thwarted in His purpose? We human beings sometimes tend to think that He was. When a plan does not work for us, we must abandon it, start over, or give it up entirely. Our possibilities and options are limited. That is not God's method. He has infinite possibilities available to Him. So we must assume that the way He chose to complete His purpose was the best and most effective.

He wanted human beings to love Him freely. He chose the way of the lover—seeking to win His rebellious creatures back to Himself. But He did not choose just any way to do it. He did not seek to win by indulging the desires of persons or by giving them special privileges. He did not choose to overlook rebellion or hostility in order to win love. Nor did He choose to use His almighty power to cow persons into accepting Him. His way was that of the ideal lover: revealing Himself to human beings in the hope that they would recognize His love for them. For those who recognize divine love cannot help responding to it.

God revealed Himself through words and deeds. He was continually doing good in order to show His love. God is good to all in some ways (such as making provision for daily life). He is good to some—those who trust him—in all ways (by giving Himself to them in love). He also revealed Himself in words. The prophets of the Old Testament proclaimed "the word of the Lord." Through them, God showed His nature and called for a response.

God's greatest—and final—revelation came in a Deed and a Word, the Word made flesh, Jesus Christ. This was "his one and only Son." Jesus completed God's revelation in several unique ways:

(1) As Son of God, He fully revealed God as Holy Love.

(2) As Son of man, He fully carried out what God expects of human beings. He proclaimed God as Heavenly Father and Ruler over the kingdom of heaven. He trusted in God completely in all circumstances. He kept God's laws perfectly. In His own self He did what God had been trying to get thousands of persons to do throughout the centuries.

(3) His obedience to God led Him to His death on the cross. There He showed what happens when Holy Love encounters evil at its worst. In so doing, He made atonement for the sins of humanity. He made it possible for all persons to be reconciled to God.

(4) His resurrection showed the triumph of Holy Love over all the forces of evil. God raised him with a spiritual body that is the prototype of the body which each believer will have at the resurrection of the dead.

In Jesus' life, death, and resurrection, He made it possible for all persons to respond to God as the Father wished. He revealed God perfectly. We have "the light of the knowledge of the glory of God [God's essential character] in the face of Christ" (2 Cor. 4:6). So we can recognize God as supreme and worship Him with total allegiance.

Also, we have evidence that God will carry out all His promises. His gift of His Son shows the length to which He will go to do good for His creatures (Rom. 8:32; 2 Cor. 1:20). We can trust Him totally for all of life, here and hereafter.

Finally, we can obey God in His ethical demands because we have the nature of Jesus within us through the new birth (Rom. 8:3-5).

God's seeking love was fulfilled in Jesus, and He has continued to seek the lost before and since that event. He does this with infinite patience. Some Christians, seeing the desperate state of the world, ponder why God does not put an end to the suffering. But God is always seeing new fields ripe to be harvested, new sheep to be gathered back into the fold, new children to be born into his family. Not all will respond. But as Peter said, "The Lord is not slow in keeping his promise [to return], . . . He is patient with you, not wanting anyone to perish, but everyone to come to repentance" (2 Peter 3:9).

God's redeeming love.—"That whoever believes in him shall not perish."

Even though God's seeking love would draw persons to Him, there would still be a problem: the continuing sinfulness of these persons. God is holy. He cannot have relationships with those who are not holy. Those who turn to Him might repent of past sins, but if they retained their sinful nature, that nature would continue to poison their lives.

Therefore God made provision for those who trusted in Him to change their nature. They could have a new birth —from spiritual death to spiritual life. To effect this and still retain human free will required a special kind of love on God's part. This was redeeming love.

In order to help human beings to a recognition of their sinful plight, and to an act of will in trusting God to change their nature, at least three things were necessary.

First was identification with their plight. We often do not understand our own condition until someone else understands it, nor do we feel that others truly understand us unless they can sympathize, even empathize, with us. So God had to find an avenue of identifying with sinful humanity.

Second was a recognition of the sinfulness of sin. People do not turn away from that which gives them satisfaction without understanding the terrible dangers in that satisfaction. They do not stop smoking or abusing their bodies with drugs or alcohol unless they understand what they are doing to their bodies. So they will not desire to turn away from sin unless they understand its terrible consequences. God wanted to show humanity the awfulness of rebellion against Him, for this is the essence of all sin.

Third was the chance to start over. Persons had to believe that they could have a new chance at life, a new nature that could be more than ordinary human beings can achieve. So God had to make possible a new birth. New life comes from death. We plant seeds which die, so that the life within them may sprout and make new plants. But human beings have no spiritual life in them. Dying could not change their nature. God had to provide for this problem—how to bring new life out of the spiritually dead persons whom He was seeking.

He accomplished all these in a single act—in sending His Son to earth. Not only did Jesus reveal the Father, He also identified with sinful humanity. He never sinned, but He came in daily contact with sin and its consequences. He learned firsthand what sin had done to the human race. Further, He showed the sinfulness of sin on the cross. There sin did its worst to the best of the universe. Nothing so fully reveals the horror of sin as the death of Jesus.

Through his death and resurrection Jesus made possible a new life for every person on earth. His death became the death through which life comes. His new life was the first example of what God can and will accomplish in the lives of all who trust in Him through Jesus Christ.

God's love is so great He was willing to go to any lengths to win human beings to Him. He was unswerving in this purpose, no matter what it cost Him. His redeeming love never fails. Throughout the ages, whoever turns to God in faith on the basis of what Jesus Christ has done, will find God faithful to His word.

Herein lies the meaning of the word *believe*. It does not mean an intellectual assent, as I might indicate I believe there are nine planets. Such a belief does not change my life! But my belief in the safety of airplanes, the healthfulness of eating the right foods, and the security of a loving husband can make all the difference in the world to me. So our belief in Jesus means a commitment of life to Him. When we believe in Him, we trust everything in our lives—yesterday, today, and all our tomorrows—to Him. Our faith in Jesus ushers in God's approval.

On the other hand, refusal to believe in Jesus is the ultimate sin and condemns us (John 3:18). God has made provision for everyone's salvation. The one who refuses to make that provision his own has no other recourse. He has chosen death rather than life, darkness, over light, his own self-will against fellowship with God. For such a person, how could there be anything but condemnation? Even God cannot and will not do anything to change that verdict. God has done His utmost. There is nothing more left for Him to do.

God's triumphant love.—"But have eternal life."

God's purpose of redemption may fail for some, but it is sure for all those who believe in Jesus. God has made provision for every person to have the greatest gift He can bestow: the gift of God's kind of life. This is eternal, spiritual, creative—a life lived in fellowship with God forever. This is what eternal life means. One who has this life will never perish. It is not possible for such a life ever to die. Through giving human beings eternal life, God is assured that His loving plan will ultimately triumph.

God's love is triumphant over all obstacles. He allowed His love to face every obstacle to it. Only by so doing could He touch the hearts of human beings and win them to Himself. How better to show His love than to send His Son to live and die in the midst of sin and sinners?

God's love is triumphant in its results. Already God rejoices over the millions who have turned to him by faith. His fellowship with all these redeemed persons gives Him joy and satisfaction. The kingdom of God is active in the world through Christian love, expressed toward God and toward other persons. Every advance of the kingdom is a victory of God's love.

Finally, God's love will be triumphant when He provides a new body for each of His children and a new heaven and earth for them to inhabit. There will be perfect love between God and human beings and within His universe, forever and forever. Then God's joy will be complete. He will see the final result of the plans He made at the beginning. He will have proved the power of His love to triumph over sin and death.

The Saving Power of God's Love
Ephesians 2:1-10

This passage is really a commentary on John 3:16. It tells the condition of lost humanity. It explains what God did in Jesus Christ for human beings, and it shows the results of God's activity.

All human beings, in their natural state, are spiritually dead (v. 1). This death comes about by human sinful actions (v. 1) and because of sinful human tendencies ("followed the ways of this world," v. 2). No person ever escapes either of these causes of spiritual death. Human nature is bent toward a life of self-will (v. 3). This self-will causes persons to think only of gratifying their own desires. The "sinful nature" with "its desires and thoughts" covers all the types of sins which human beings commit. It includes laziness as well as intemperance, spite as well as murder, greed as well as illicit sex.

Because human beings are so totally steeped in the "sin principle," they are all objects of God's wrath. We will study about God's wrath in the chapter on God's forgiveness. Now it is sufficient to point out that the only outcome for such a life is death and destruction. No one who lives in this way can be said to have spiritual life. The whole world of sinful persons is like a group of skeletons, walking around decked in beautiful clothes but dead all the same.

But "God so loved"! Verse 4 shows the true depth and

breadth of God's love. He is "rich in mercy." He is a
billionaire when it comes to showing mercy to persons
who have done nothing to deserve it.

Verse 5 tells what he does to show his mercy. Here are
"dry bones," with no life left in them. But God makes
them alive—not just physically alive as one would raise
somebody from the dead. His gift is a new kind of life:
spiritual, eternal life, the kind of life which Christ Himself now has. Jesus was raised with an eternal body because this was His by right. But those who believe in Jesus
are given spiritual life as a gift from God. This is the
ultimate demonstration of God's grace.

Verse 6 goes even further. Not only are believers given
spiritual life. They are granted an exalted place in heaven,
along with Christ. Of course, this has not happened yet
in our experience. But when God decrees a happening, it
is as if it were already in effect. The verbs *made alive,raised,*
and *seated* all express action that has taken place once and
for all. In God's eyes His children not only have life, but
they have been identified with Christ and been given a
place of honor with Him. Therefore, these things are true.
We have only to wait for them to be completed in our
experience.

Why did God do all these things for dead creatures? In
order to show what a billionaire of grace He is! He could
have transported us from death to life but assigned us a
low position in His eternal economy. But this is not His
plan. When He forgives, He forgives all the way. (Read
Ps. 103:11-12.) When He gives eternal life, His gifts are
without reservation. When He blesses, His blessings are
incomparable.

This is the gift of God (v. 8). It comes by His grace, and
it is received through faith in His promise. He has prom-

ised to accept all who trust in Jesus Christ. It requires faith
to believe this, and faith is needed.

We might compare this requirement to an invitation to
step onto an airplane. Those who believed that the plane
would carry them from one destination to another would
board the plane; those who did not believe would remain
on the ground. Only those who acted on faith would
reach the faraway city. It would take no special knowledge of aerodynamics to board the plane. It would take no
particular strength. No one would be excluded—except
those who excluded themselves through unbelief. So it is
with our acceptance of God's gift of grace.

Faith excludes works (v. 9). No one has to do anything
to win God's favor. In fact, no one can do anything. Who
can expect spiritually dead persons to act? If they could,
they still could not do enough to merit God's favor. "The
ground is level at the cross," as I have heard it put. God's
love makes it possible for persons to be saved on the same
basis—by faith alone.

But there is a place for works (v. 10). We are God's
"workmanship." This word means something made or
created. There are other translations of this word: "handiwork" (NEB) or "design." But I like best the translation
of *The Jerusalem Bible:* "We are God's work of art." That is
beautiful! It says I am not just a piece of pottery or a
simple wood carving, tossed out casually by the Master
Artisan. I am one of His masterpieces! Of course, I know
that God makes nothing that is not worthy of Him. But
it is hard for me to think of myself in that manner. "God's
work of art" presents me a sense of my worth in His sight.

Also, to be "God's work of art" means to act. We are
not like paintings to be hung in art galleries or books to
be read passively. We are more like plays or symphonies
—to be performed. Reading a play or the score of a sym-

phony is not satisfying to most people. An interpretation by a living person is needed. So God, in a way, has prepared a script for me to perform. I am His partner in the script writing, as well as in the performing. I can determine much of what goes into the play. But I am the one to put it into action.

So God has created each one of us anew, in order that we will do "good works." God has planned for these in advance. This is part of living in His kingdom. His plan is for each Christian to put into action the laws of His kingdom. Each Christian is to mirror forth in day-by-day life the character of God so that others will be drawn to Him. We are to be "salt" and "light." Thus, God's plan for His world is being furthered daily by those who accept His Son as Savior.

GOD'S LOVE AND YOUR RESPONSE

First John 4:19 says, "We love because he first loved us." We learn from God what love is; we learn to live in love because of the love God sheds upon us. God asks of us, in return for His boundless love, that we love Him.

To love God means to obey Him, not only to talk and sing about our love for him (1 John 3:23). And how do we obey God? By loving our Christian brothers and sisters and showing this love in action (1 John 3:16-18).

Have you been thrilled anew at the thought of God's love for you? Would you like to show a worthy response to that love? You can do it simply. You can express concrete love and concern for others each day. You can begin with those who are in your "family of faith"—those who have been born anew as you have. You can expand that care and concern to all around you.

Think of the many ways you can show love for others in your actions: caring for the sick, giving to the poor and hungry, comforting the sorrowing, congratulating those who are rejoicing. Read Romans 12:4-18 and Matthew 25:31-40. You will find in these verses enough love-in-action to keep you going for a long while.

6.

God Is Faithful
to His Holiness

As I have pointed out, God's plan for winning persons to Him was to reveal Himself as Holy Love. We have explored the meaning of the word *love*. Now we need to deal with the word *holy*. It is a far more difficult task because holiness is unfamiliar to us. I confess that I was vague on this subject when I began to study it. I still do not understand it well, but I know more about it than when I started! I hope that this will be true of you as well.

The word *holy* is used far more often than it is understood. We sing, "Holy, holy, holy! Lord God Almighty!" We pray to the "Holy Trinity," and we know that the "Holy Spirit" is the Third Person of the Trinity. We likewise know that Jesus is the Second Person. But these uses of the word do not give us many clues to its meaning.

Perhaps the reason the word is so vague is that it means "wholly other." To be holy means to be set apart, to be different. How do we identify with that idea in our daily living? How do we, surrounded by a material world, relate to what is absolutely spiritual? We can think about heaven as being holy. We can know about holy angels and

76

about God's name being holy. We affirm that the Bible is holy.

So the idea of God as Holy Love can present what seems to be a contradiction. As Love He is seen as close to us, relating to us, like us in Jesus Christ. But as Holy, He is far away from us. He is so different from us that we have no way of describing Him. Yet he calls us to be like him—"be holy, because I am holy" (1 Pet. 1:16).

Here, then, is where our understanding of God's holiness is important to us in everyday living. God calls us to be holy, as He is. What does this mean? How can we hope to live up to His holiness?

People seem to take two opposite stands on this matter. Some Christians emphasize God's otherness. They claim it is impossible to be like Him. So they do not even try. They reserve to heaven all references to being like God. It cannot be done perfectly in this life, they seem to say. So let us make no effort at all.

Other Christians make being holy a matter of pride, of glorying in their differences from "lesser" Christians. Some speak of a "second blessing," an anointing of the Holy Spirit that makes it possible for them to live "above" the world. Some of them even talk about "sinless perfection" as a state which Christians can attain in this life.

I once knew a family who made this claim. The mother was a proud woman who was always pulling her children away from the "contamination" of other Christian young people. One day she indulged in what I would have called, in anyone else, a "fit of temper."

That night, at a youth group meeting, she was again making her claim to being "sinlessly perfect." I asked her about her outburst. She turned to me and heatedly declared that what I had seen had nothing to do with her "perfection." "That was an error of the head, not the heart," she explained. "God knows my heart, and He knows that I did not mean to be angry. So He doesn't hold it against me, and you shouldn't either. My heart is always right with God."

I am not relating this incident to cast any ridicule upon the woman. Rather, I wish to show the lengths to which people may go in order to claim special privileges for themselves before God. (It is interesting to notice that this woman never apologized to the people to whom she had expressed her anger.)

The question of everyday holiness still remains. If we are not to postpone holiness till heaven, and if we are not to seek a "special" kind of holiness, how can we be holy as God is holy?

We have seen that holy means to be "wholly other." The word also refers to character. Our word *holy* is related to the word *whole*. These words in English are derived from ancient English and German words meaning "complete" or "sound, healthy." In this sense God is the only complete being in the universe. He is one with Himself. All the elements of His nature are in harmony with one another. So He is holy in two senses: He is all that He should be, and He is different entirely from us, with our contradictions and changes.

When we declare that God is "faithful to His holiness," we mean that God is faithful to Himself. He will always do right by us. He will not change His purpose for human beings, no matter what they do. He will be faithful to His promises. God's holiness can be trusted.

Also, God is faithful in that He will not allow His holiness to be ignored. No one can rebel against God's righteous laws and get away with it. God demands holy living from those whom His holiness and love have touched.

So we can depend on God's holiness to ensure that He will have the right relationship with humankind. At the same time we need to make a commitment to seek right relations ourselves, not only with Him but with our human brothers and sisters. When God said, "Be ye holy, because I am holy," He was asking for this kind of commitment. He was asking His people to recognize His holiness and to seek the same kind of holiness, even though it would not come anywhere close to His. The only person ever to do that was Jesus Christ, and He is the God-man. He is our example and our means of encouragement as we seek to be God's kind of people. This is what it means for us to be holy.

Our Bible study will show more of what is involved in the holiness of God and what this means for our daily living.

The Just God Who Justifies
Romans 3:21-26

How can God be both just and the One who justifies? This question expresses the mystery of the ages. The first two chapters of Romans are filled with explanations about how God's righteousness shows itself toward sinning humanity. God is the judge who condemns all for their rebellion against Him. Even those who tried to keep the law of Moses, failed. For to keep all the law and yet transgress at one point is to be a lawbreaker. "Whoever keeps the whole law and yet stumbles at just one point is guilty of breaking all of it" (Jas. 2:10).

But God's righteousness is not expressed simply in judgment. Romans 3:21 speaks of "a righteousness from God, apart from law." This righteousness is God's determination to "do right" by His sinning creatures. He is going to provide a right standing for those who have no rights. He is going to declare innocent those whom He has already declared guilty. And He is going to make it possible for these sinners to so live that they will have His righteous quality of life. This righteousness has to be "apart from law" because the law was never able to produce truly righteous living (see v. 20).

This is not a "talking-about" righteousness. God's plan is worked out through life. In this case He worked through the life, death, and resurrection of Jesus Christ. Faith in Him is the means God has chosen to bring sinning humanity into a right relationship with Himself.

This is one of the glorious facets of God's plan for saving human beings. Suppose a person had to have special knowledge or to be born into a special group of people or to have a certain amount of wealth (or lack of it) in order to be saved. In every case, many persons would be excluded from God's gift of salvation. But God has made faith the avenue to Himself. So "There is no difference" between persons (v. 22). All have sinned, and all are "justified freely" (v. 24).

It is sometimes tempting to look at persons and try to measure the depths of their sin. One may think, *Well, I've never done anything like that person.* Or another may feel that he or she does not have as much to repent of as a certain person. So coming to Jesus, for such a one, may not seem as earth-shaking and life-changing.

But the fact is that "all . . . fall short of the glory of God" (v. 23). When we look at sin in this light, we realize that everyone is included. Falling short of the glory of God means not measuring up to His goodness, His holiness. God does not expect us to be holy to the same degree that He is. But He does expect the same quality of life from those who are made in His image. How far short we fall of His goodness!

Measured, from this perspective, the various "degrees" of sin that we imagine in us and other people are wiped out. A person standing on a plot of ground may be able to see variations in it—molehills or indentations that are noticeable. But to a person in a helicopter five hundred feet above the ground, these variations are not apparent. The plot looks level. So it is with our falling short of God's glory. From His perspective we are all on the same level. All sin is sin toward God.

There is also "no difference" in the possibility of our receiving his grace. God has concluded everyone equally under judgment so He can include everyone equally under grace. In a court of law, the judge has to act in accordance with law. If the defendant is found guilty, the judge has to sentence him. He cannot set the defendant free, but God acts in accordance with His own will. He recognizes our actions as sin. But He renders His verdict in line with His love for us. This is grace!

How can He do this? "Through the redemption that came by Christ Jesus" (v. 24). The word *redemption* is the translation of a Greek word meaning "liberation," often used of the price paid to free a slave. Paul was evidently referring to the fact that God's grace is not cheap. It is costly. Some people may wonder why God did not just issue an edict that all sinners could come to Him without repentance and faith. God could have decided to bypass the death of His Son on the cross. But those who think in that vein are wrong. Jesus' death on the cross made at least two points eternally clear: It showed the awful character of sin and revealed the eternal value of a human soul.

This redemption is the keystone of God's plan of salvation. Verse 25 says that "God presented him as a sacrifice of atonement." This was not something Jesus did all alone while the Father and the Holy Spirit ignored it. "God was reconciling the world to himself in Christ" (2 Cor. 5:19). So God "presented" Him or "put Him forward" for all the world to see.

Jesus was presented as a "sacrifice of atonement" (v. 25). These ideas are all difficult for us to understand. There is a mystery at the heart of Jesus' atonement which no one—great theologian or simple follower of Christ—can ever penetrate. But we must do our best to understand what we can of it.

In the Old Testament the "sacrifice of atonement" referred to the sacrifice made on behalf of the Israelites on the Day of Atonement. An animal was slaughtered, and its blood was sprinkled inside the Holy of Holies. The death of the animal was a token of the penalty for sin against the Lord. The blood symbolized life. Sprinkling it in the Holy of Holies indicated that a life had been given for the sins of the people.

Jesus' sacrifice is often referred to as "substitutionary atonement." One way to understand this is to think of ourselves being put in His place. In the Old Testament, the sinners might imagine themselves in the place of the animal sacrificed for their sins. They might think of the terrible penalty that was appropriate to their sins. They would repent of their sins as they realized that they deserved to die, but God was allowing them to make a sacrifice instead. In His graciousness, He wiped the sinful slate clean! So once a year the people of Israel had a new start. The instructions about the Day of Atonement say: "On this day atonement will be made for you, to cleanse you. Then, before the Lord, you will be clean from all your sins" (Lev. 16:30).

This sacrifice had to be made every year. But Jesus came

to substitute Himself, once and for all, for sinful human beings.

"Faith in His blood" means to trust that what God has promised to do through Jesus Christ, He will do. God was willing to cleanse His people Israel from sin upon the sacrifice of an animal. Certainly He is faithful to cleanse every person from sin upon the sacrifice of Jesus Christ, God's only Son. For God does more than forgive the sins of those who trust in Jesus. He draws those persons into a right relationship with Him. Those who have been enemies, He now calls His friends. Those who have been rebellious, He now accepts as His obedient children. Those who have been dead, He makes alive.

The result of this changed standing with God is that we now can live out the status God has so freely bestowed upon us. We can be His friends, His children, His new creation, in actual fact as well as in His decision. He makes it possible for us to grow into His holiness, beginning in this life. This holy image of God will not be completed until there is a new heaven and a new earth. But He gives us all that we need to begin and to make progress on the journey of holiness.

The Demands of the Holy God
Micah 6:6-8

This passage is set within a "court case" between the Lord and Israel. The Lord accused His people of sinning against Him and forgetting their covenant with Him. The people answered by stating that they had kept the religious rituals which God prescribed for them. They felt that God was being unreasonable. But then God told them what He truly requires, and it was far different from what they had imagined. Verses 6-7 give the people's request for God's requirement, and verse 8 is God's answer.

The people felt that they had done what the law required of them in ritual. They wanted to know how much more the Lord demanded. If He wanted burnt offerings, they were willing to give Him more. They became extravagant in their questions. Did God want thousands of animals slaughtered for their sins? Should they furnish enough oil that it would flow from the altar in rivers? They even suggested child sacrifice. God never demanded such, but the pagans around Israel regularly sacrificed their children. If God were so demanding, Israel implied, perhaps He wanted their children in atonement for the people's sins.

God's answer through the prophet was both a reminder and a rebuke. God stated that His requirement was nothing new. He had been demanding that from the beginning. It was Israel who had strayed, not God who was changing His requirement.

The word *man* in Hebrew refers to the whole race of humankind as we would use the word *humanity*. "What is good" refers to what is good for *all* human beings. God's requirement of His people is no different from His desires for all persons. To carry out God's requirement is to live truly human. God does not make arbitary demands; his desire is for the good of human beings. His laws are directed toward that end.

There are three parts to God's requirement. The first is to "act justly" (v. 8). The word *justly* means to "do right." Those who act accordingly will keep the Golden Rule. They will be considerate of the rights and needs of others, no matter whether or not these persons have a special relationship with them.

The second part is to "love mercy" (v. 8). This word in

the Hebrew refers to the obligations which come from special relationships—to the duties between husband and wife, between parents and children, even where there are no laws to govern their actions. The word *mercy* is often used of God's dealings with the people of His covenant. So this requirement goes further than the first. It covers the mutual loyalties that persons bound in covenant with one another should have. For Christians it means the deep love, loyalty, concern, and self-giving that all children of God owe to one another.

The third part of the requirement is to "walk humbly with your God" (v. 8). Throughout the Bible the word *walk* is regularly used to mean life-style or manner of life—daily living. As we saw in our study of Romans 3, there is no human merit by which we can approach God. We must come to Him in humility, aware of our own unworthiness. Our daily lives in His presence must reflect the same humility. Only in that spirit may human beings have fellowship with the holy God.

God's Provision for Our Holiness
1 Corinthians 6:19; Galatians 5:16-18, 22-25

The summary of God's demands in Micah 6:8 is easy to understand but hard to follow. In fact, all the demands of righteous living are impossible for human beings to carry out, but God has made provision for the holiness of those persons saved by His grace.

He has done this by sending His Holy Spirit to live within each one of us. The Spirit is our birthright, sent into our hearts at the time of our new birth. Therefore, the Christian's body is spoken of as "a temple of the Holy Spirit" (1 Cor. 6:19). Anywhere that God dwells is a temple. What a tremendous privilege—that God will choose to make His dwelling with us!

I once heard a preacher observe that the greatest surprise in the world is not that God would live in the person of Jesus Christ: Jesus was and is pure, holy, and loving. The greatest surprise is that God would choose to live in me, sinful and dirty and crooked as I am! But this is how He has chosen to make me holy.

The Spirit within us does many things for us. He helps us to pray, gives us guidance and encouragement, helps us to know the will of God, teaches us about Christ, and more. Our main concern here is how He helps us to become holy.

Two elements are needed—the working of the Spirit and the consent of our wills. To "live by the Spirit" (Gal. 5:16) means constantly to be determined to follow the Spirit's guidance, which is not easy. There is a tug of war going on in our personalities between the "desires of the sinful nature" and the Spirit. When we are born from above, we have a new nature at the center of our beings. But the nature we were born with still exists. There is a constant struggle between these two. Often we may feel ourselves torn to pieces in the struggle.

If we keep thinking about living by law, we are under constant temptation to break that law. "But if you are led by the Spirit, you are not under law" (Gal. 5:18). Have you ever tried to get rid of an idea or stop a habit by continually determining not to keep on doing it? Then you know how hard it is to avoid the temptation. This is what the law does. It constantly reminds us of what we must avoid. It is like trying to keep from running a red light by thinking of not running the light. It becomes almost an obsession to see whether you can run the light without getting caught. But if you concentrate on stopping when you should, the idea of running the light does not bother you.

So, if we are led by the Spirit, our thinking is changed. We concentrate on God's goodness, not on our sinfulness. We let the Holy Spirit guide us. We do not try to be righteous through legalistically changing ourselves.

How then does the Spirit make us holy? By cultivating in us the qualities of life which lead to holiness. These are called "the fruit of the Spirit" (v. 22). Look at these qualities.

There is *love*, the ability to care for others in the same way God does. There is *joy*. This is a bubbling up of the springs of happiness, based on a conviction that life is in the final analysis good, and that God's kingdom will be the final victor. There is *peace*. This is the kind of peace Jesus made possible: a right relationship with God, and therefore right relationships with other persons.

There is also *patience*. This means to have a "long temper," not a short fuse. There is *kindness*, an attitude of consideration for others. There is, along with it, *goodness*, actions that show kind attitudes and that "do right" by others.

There is *faithfulness*, the quality of loyalty to a trust, the ability to keep a promise. There is *gentleness*, which refers to the strength that does not need to be aggressive. The gentle person is teachable, ready to allow others their "place in the sun," unwilling to squander strength on having his own way at all times. Finally there is *self-control*. This is the power to use one's will to conquer one's immediate desires.

Put these qualities of life alongside the demands of holiness in Micah 6:8—justice, mercy, and a humble walk with God. Could these demands be met without such qualities? Don't these qualities make it possible to meet the demands of holiness? Every quality is desirable if persons wish to live in harmony with one another and

with God. The Holy Spirit gently, persistently, unceas-
ingly cultivates these within the life of every Christian.
There is no law against them. They are good for every
human being.

How do we cooperate with the Spirit in His work of
producing holiness within us? We reckon that our sinful
nature is dead (v. 24). The basis of all sin is putting ourselves first. Whenever we determine not to do this, we are
crucifying our selfishness. We "have crucified" our sinful
nature, but it is not yet dead! It continues to plague us. But
when it does, we can look toward the cross of Christ. In
His death we died. In His new life we are made alive. The
Spirit within us is the proof of our new nature.

We live by the Spirit—that is a fact. It is our constant
task to "keep in step" with him. This is a military term.
It means to march in "synch." This calls for effort. It
means subordinating our wills to the person who sets the
pace. If the Holy Spirit sets the pace for our lives, it is our
business to march in step with Him. Whenever we fall out
of step, we need not stop to beat our heads in frustration
at our failure. We need instead to fall back into step and
march on!

YOUR RESPONSE TO GOD'S HOLINESS

Consider God as the "wholly other," the One who is
pure spirit, the One who is total and consistent Goodness.
What should be your response to this Supreme Being?

First there should be *awe* and *reverence.* The Bible speaks
of this as "the fear of the Lord" (Ps. 19:9). The word *fear*
does not mean dread or panic. It means a reverent awe.
Such a response implies that human beings should bow in
the presence of the holy God. They should acknowledge
Him as their Maker, Creator, Master, and King. "The fear
of the Lord," the Bible says, "is the beginning of knowl-

edge" (Prov. 1:7). The wisdom we need for living life today and in all our tomorrows comes from this acknowledgment of God as supreme in our lives.

Second, there should be *praise.* Think what it would mean in our lives not to have a holy God over us. His holiness should call forth hosannas and hallelujahs, joy and singing. Worship services should be filled with both awe and praise. The major purpose of the Christian, alone or when gathered with other Christians, is to worship God. The more we see of God to worship, the deeper will be our fellowship with Him. The more we worship and adore Him, the more we grow to be like Him through Jesus Christ. It is as if God were a huge fountain spraying everything around it with the water of life. The closer we come to this fountain, the more of that life touches us. But the farther away we stray from the fountain, the less of that life we experience.

This is the third response—a continual *striving to grow* into God's holiness. This will involve yielding to the Spirit's guidance. It will mean being more aware of our falling "short of the glory of God" (Rom. 3:23). It will mean repenting of sins and turning away from them. It will mean seeking every day to show evidence of the "fruit of the Spirit" (v. 22).

Will you make these three suggestions matters of daily prayer for the next week? Ask God to let you see where and how you need to change daily life so you will be more attuned to His holiness. Do you need to feel more awe and reverence toward Him? Do you need to make more opportunities to praise Him for His holiness? Do you need to yield yourself more firmly to the Spirit's leading and to His cultivation of holy qualities in your life?

You need not make life-changing decisions all at once.

One step toward God is all He asks of you. But He does ask that you continue to take one more step, and then one more step, so you will keep on moving toward being a mature Christian.

7.

God Is Faithful
to His Covenant

Let me pause here to recap the previous six chapters. God had a plan for His world. He created it to show His power and to reflect His nature. He produced His highest creatures, human beings, to share this world with Him and to adore Him for His power, love, and goodness. As an old confession of faith puts it: "The chief end of man is to glorify God and enjoy Him forever."

God did not want His creatures to be robots, incapable of any other response except total obedience. So He gave human beings free will. Alone among His creation, persons were able to answer yes or no to God. If they were to "glorify God and enjoy Him forever," they must do so willingly. They were free to accept or reject, to obey or to rebel. We well recognize that the history of humankind is far more rebellion than acceptance. But God has continued to woo human beings to Him.

He did this by revealing Himself as Holy Love. This revelation was designed to cause persons to love Him in return and to desire to live for Him. The responses which God desires were defined as:

(1) Total allegiance to God as Supreme Being

(2) Faith in God's ability and willingness to keep His promises

(3) Obedience to God's will and moral demands

These responses were made concrete by means of a covenant. We have already seen God's side of the covenant: his unconditional and unbreakable promises. But if He were not going to change His mind about these promises, why was a covenant needed? Because He understood human nature! The human will is bent toward selfishness and self-concern. A covenant was a tangible method for human beings to keep their selfish tendencies from overwhelming their desires to love and serve God.

This kind of covenant has many of the elements of marital vows. Two people who make such vows have usually expressed their promises to each other as their relationship has deepened. Why, then, the necessity of open vows? This was one of the "pet" questions of the 1970s—if two people love each other, why should they need "a piece of paper" or vows made in the presence of others? A good answer to this question was unconsciously given by a woman who declared that two people should not promise to love each other "till death do us part." Love, she noted, cannot be guaranteed. Two people cannot pledge that they will love each other for the rest of their lives. And if love goes, then the marriage goes.

Love, to her, was an emotion, and emotions do change —but love, to God, is commitment and action. He loves human beings; therefore, He is committed to them and to their highest welfare. He expects the same kind of commitment from those who respond to Him. Loving God means to live out the three responses He calls for.

The need for commitment is often seen more easily

under the old covenant than under the new. We can see that the people needed to obey God's will in order to continue to enjoy His favor. But what about us—who live under "the new covenant in my blood," as Jesus expressed it (Luke 22:20)? There seems to be no need for us to make a covenant with God. We are saved through the blood of Christ. God's grace will never pass away from us.

This kind of thinking, unfortunately, seems to pervade many of the sermons and the teachings we receive. We hear much said about "accepting Jesus as personal Savior." Little is mentioned—and usually not in the same context—about *at the same time* accepting him as Lord of our lives. We call Jesus our "Savior and Lord." But too often we do not think about what the word *Lord* means.

The early Christians had no misconceptions about this word. To them it meant a total and absolute ruler. A similar meaning was "master," the owner of slaves. A master had absolute control of the lives he owned, even the power of life and death. When have you heard the word *Lord* explained in such a way? Do you think of Jesus as having total power over your life so that every action and thought should be under His command?

When I was a seminary student, I had a disturbing encounter with a minister. He declared to me that people could declare, "Christ is the Son of God," and believe whatever they wanted to about that statement. "You can believe that Jesus is the only Son of God," he commented to me. "And I can believe that Jesus is a son of God just as we are children of God. It doesn't make any difference how you interpret the statement." But it made a world of difference to me, and I said so. If Jesus were not the only Son of God, then He could not be my Savior.

I was scandalized by this man's beliefs, and probably you are, too. But it is also scandalous to say, "Jesus is

Lord," and let it mean whatever we want it to mean. If Jesus is Savior, He is also Lord. That is the covenant we make with Him. It is a covenant of grace, not of keeping laws, but the obligations upon us are just as binding as they were on the people of Israel. Further, the responses God expected from them—giving supreme loyalty to Him, trusting Him in all areas of life, and obeying His will in all facets of life—are required of us as well.

Let us in our Bible study explore the covenants God made in the Old Testament and see how these are expanded and deepened in the New Testament. We will study the covenant with Abraham, the covenant with Israel, and the covenant with David.

Abraham, the Man of God
Genesis 15:1-6; Romans 4:3,16-24

The first covenant which involved a response to God was made with Abraham. The first statement of this covenant is found in Genesis 12:1-3. God made certain unconditional promises to Abraham. He asked for an act of faith in response. He told Abraham to leave his country and his father's house, to be a wanderer in a strange land. At no time did God demand that Abraham show himself to be worthy of God's favor. The act of obedient faith followed God's promises rather than preceding them. God's choice of Abraham was purely an act of grace, to be accepted in faith.

There are several other statements of God's covenant with Abraham: Genesis 15; 17; 22. In each confirmation, God made plainer what He intended to do for Abraham. Abraham took further steps of faith and obedience with each renewal of the covenant. Genesis 15:1-6 illustrates the way Abraham showed his faith in God. It explains why he is "the father" of the faithful (Rom. 4:16).

Abraham was evidently in deep need of reassurance from God at that time. The Lord spoke to him in a vision, urging him not to be afraid. As we see further on, Abraham was in the grip of doubt and uncertainty. God did not at first relieve his doubts. Instead, God offered Himself to Abraham.

This is an important lesson which needs to be stressed over and over: God's best answer to our fears, doubts, misfortunes, and sorrows is not the relief of these troubles. He offers, not a respite, but Himself. With Him on our side, no trouble is big enough to engulf us.

God reminded Abraham that He Himself was Abraham's shield against trouble, His reward no matter what happened.

Abraham's reply showed his distress and also his close relationship with God. He complained that the Lord had not fulfilled His promise of children (Gen. 12:2). Abraham was—like all of us—making His own plans. God had not acted; so Abraham had (15:2-3). He had set up the machinery to transfer his estate to a servant.

God's response was swift and overpowering. He reassured Abraham that he would have many descendants. There would be an infinite number, as impossible to count as the stars of the heavens and the sands along the seashore.

Abraham's response was exactly the right one: "Abraham believed the Lord" (v. 6). He stopped acting in his own behalf. He put his trust in the Lord, and the Lord "credited it to him as righteousness."

Two words in this phrase could stand explanation. "Credited" is an accounting word. It means to add to one's account on the credit side. "Righteousness" means the kind of behavior called for in a relationship of trust, as among relatives. God took Abraham's faith and made it stand for right behavior toward Himself. It did not matter whether Abraham acted perfectly toward God at all times. His faith "filled the bill." This phrase becomes clearer to us as we study it in Romans 4:16-24.

Paul quoted Genesis 15:6 in Romans 4:3. He spent much of the rest of the chapter explaining what God had done. The Jews considered that they alone were children of Abraham. Paul declared that the promise of God was given to those who would accept it in faith. Therefore, all who gave to God the same faith as Abraham did were his offspring. "He is the father of us all" (v. 16).

This is the way God fulfilled His promise to Abraham that he should be "father of many nations" (v. 17). This is another valuable lesson for us. God's promises are always fulfilled far beyond human imagining. To have limited Abraham's offspring to only his physical descendants would have diminished God's promise. But to make every person eligible to be a child of Abraham through faith in God is to make that offspring innumerable.

What was the quality of Abraham's faith which made it so appropriate in God's sight? It was not that Abraham's faith never wavered. Genesis 15:1-6 makes that clear. It was the way Abraham recognized Who God is and what He can do. This corresponds to Hebrews 11:6. Faith must believe that God exists, and that He will do what He has promised. So Abraham believed in God as One who could bring life out of death and create something out of nothingness. This understanding of God is essential for any relationship with Him.

Romans 4:18-21 describes Abraham's faith further. "Against all hope, Abraham in hope believed." These two "hopes" are different. The first was man's hope. Abraham and Sarah had hoped for years to have children. Now both he and Sarah were far beyond child-bearing years (v.

19). The only hope left to Abraham was a divine hope—the belief that God could work when human power could not.

In this faith Abraham "gave glory to God, being fully persuaded that God had power to do what he had promised" (vv. 20-21). How did Abraham give "glory" to God? By recognizing Who God is and dealing with Him accordingly.

It requires faith to do this. So God credited Abraham's faith to him as righteousness (v. 22). Any act which tries to elevate human worth and human ability to fend for oneself is not righteousness. Only submission to God as supreme can be an act of right relationship with Him—which is righteousness.

"Here was a man who took the right way to receive sovereign blessing. . . . He treated the Promiser as what He is, all-sufficient and all-faithful. He opened his empty hand in that persuasion, and so, because the hand was empty, the blessing was laid upon its palm."[1]

Abraham's act of faith was credited as righteousness in yet another sense. He had taken the first step in right relationship with God. Therefore, God viewed all Abraham's actions as being in right relationship with Him. We saw in the chapter on God's purpose that what He declares to be so is so, because He can make it so. So, he could make Abraham righteous on the basis of the man's belief in God's promise and power.

The same transaction holds good for all persons who take God at His word—including us (vv. 23-24). We have to believe God when we have no proof that He will do what He says. We have to recognize Him as the living God who brings life out of death and creates out of nothingness. But we have an even better basis on which to believe than Abraham did. He believed that God would create new life in Sarah's womb in spite of their advanced ages. But we recognize that God has created new life out of death through the resurrection of Jesus Christ. Abraham had to look forward in faith and hope to the birth of Isaac. We look backward in faith and joy to the resurrection of our Lord. Thus, all of us who believe in Jesus Christ are part of the covenant God made with Abraham.

But God did not stop with individuals in his making of covenants. He made a corporate covenant with a whole group of people—a nation.

Israel, the People of God
Exodus 19:3-8; 1 Peter 2:9-10

Why did God need to make a covenant with a whole group of people? Because faith is hard to hold in isolation. A company of believers has greater strength than solitary persons who are faithful. Missionaries in isolated areas often testify how difficult it is to maintain strong faith when surrounded by pagans.

Further, a group of believers makes a more profound impact in witnessing to others than only one person can. A group can show how loyalty to God, belief in His promises, and obedience to His will work out in relationships. This was the purpose for which God chose a nation: to demonstrate how belief in the one true God changes lives and produces right relationships between persons. (Recall Mic. 6:8 in the discussion on the holiness of God.)

The descendants of Jacob (Israel) had lived in Egypt for about four hundred years when God appeared to Moses. They had become an enslaved people, oppressed by the Egyptians and forced into hard manual labor. Then God came to deliver them. He showed His power through the plagues sent on Egypt. He saved them from the Egyptian army at the Red Sea. He guided them through the wilderness, providing them with food and water. Finally they arrived at Mount Sinai. There God made His covenant with the people.

Notice that, just as with Abraham, God called His people to covenant *before* He had fulfilled all His promises to them. In both cases God was asking for a faithful response. It would have been easy for Abraham and the Israelites to respond to God *after* they had seen His promises fulfilled. But that was not God's way. Human beings need to respond to Him by believing in His power even before it is fully demonstrated.

However, God did not demand a response before He had acted. He had done all His mighty works in Egypt and the wilderness without asking for anything from the people. It was on the basis of His mighty acts that He called for a response from Israel.

He described His actions as being like those of a parent eagle. The eaglets, when they first began to fly, or if they fell out of the aerie, would be rescued by one of their parents. The adult eagle would swoop down, lift the eaglet onto its mighty wings, and carry the small bird back to the safety of the aeris. God used this image to show His power and also His parentlike care of the people.

He did not ask Israel to enter into covenant with an unknown God. He had shown them enough of His power and love to enable them to trust Him for the future. He asked them for two things: "Obey me fully and keep my covenant" (v. 5). To do so would require supreme allegiance to God and total trust in Him. God has always sought these responses to the revelation of Himself.

God immediately made tremendous promises to the people. They already knew that they were to receive the land promised to Abraham (Ex. 3:15-17; compare Gen. 12:6-7). Now God promised even more: they were to be

His "treasured possession," "a kingdom of priests and a holy nation." All these phrases are strategic.

The Hebrew term for "treasured possession" means the private treasure of kings. The king owned everything in his realm, but what was especially his, his private fortune, was termed his "treasured possession." So God declared that "the whole earth" belonged to Him, but He had selected Israel to be His particular treasure.

The "kingdom of priests" means a nation of priests. (All nations in that day were kingdoms.) Priests were supposed to stand between God and persons who could not approach God for themselves. The nation of Israel had their priesthood appointed by God, but they had a special relationship to God themselves. So for them to be a "kingdom of priests" implied a special mission. Their task was to interpret God to the heathen nations surrounding them, to act as priests between these people and God. This is the task which we today call "evangelism."

Israel was also to be "a holy nation." We have already discussed what such holiness involves. God intended for His people to imitate Him in being set apart from other nations and in having right dealings with one another.

Moses delivered God's word to the people, calling on them either to accept or reject God's covenant. With one voice they responded, "We will do everything the Lord has said" (v. 8). So God's covenant was confirmed with His people.

Unfortunately, the people did not continue to keep their covenant with God. The story of the Old Testament depicts how the people of Israel departed from the covenant.

Because they did not heed God's warnings, they were carried into Exile, but God had not forgotten His covenant. After two generations, a remnant returned to the

Land of Promise. But they still did not carry out the purpose for which God had chosen them. They were willing to be a "holy nation," but they refused to act as a "kingdom of priests." They would not spread the word of the Lord to the heathen peoples around them.

God gave His chosen people one more chance: He sent His only Son to them. He was their Messiah, the One promised through the centuries. He would have led them to complete God's purpose for them, but they rejected Him.

What then happened to God's covenant with a whole people? Was His purpose thwarted because Israel refused to carry out His plan for them? Certainly not! God expanded His covenant with a people to include all the Gentiles (read Rom. 9—11; Eph. 2:11-22; 1 Cor. 12:12-13). All Christians are joined in "the body of Christ" (1 Cor. 12:27) and this body made up of many diverse members is now the chosen people of God.

One evidence for this assertion is found in 1 Peter 2:9-10. Peter was writing to "God's elect" (1 Pet. 1:1). These were Christians living in various parts of Asia Minor. Some of them were Jews; many others were Gentiles. But they all belonged to Christ through God's choice of them. What did Peter say to them in 2:9? He repeated the very words God had spoken to Israel on Mount Sinai! Christians are the "new Israel" of God. The nation of Israel was the corporate group who enjoyed God's favor. The church of Jesus Christ, His body, is the corporate group which is now God's treasured possession.

Peter also pointed out the responsibility to which these new chosen people were called: to "declare the praises of him who called you out of darkness into his wonderful light." As we saw in studying Matthew 5:16, the purpose of light is to point people to God. We are to be a "nation of priests," witnessing to the grace of God in Jesus Christ. So we fulfill the purpose for which God first chose a people.

David and the Kingdom of God
2 Samuel 7:8-9,12-13; Colossians 1:13-14

From the beginning of Israel's history as a nation, it was supposed to be a theocracy. That is, its leader or king was to be God. He spoke to the people through persons whom He had chosen, but the people grew tired of not having a king. They asked for "a king to lead us, such as all the other nations have" (1 Sam. 8:5).

God agreed to their request. Yet, He was still to be supreme. He expected the king, no less than the people, to keep His covenant.

The first king, Saul, failed to do that. God then "sought out a man after his own heart and appointed him leader of his people" (1 Sam. 13:14). This was David. God was so pleased with David that He made David a special promise: "the throne of his kingdom" would be established "forever" (2 Sam. 7:8-9,12-13).

How could God have kept that promise? There has been no Jewish kingdom since the Babylonian Exile. But God's promise has been kept, and it is in force today! David's kingdom was not His but God's. That kingdom has been established forever. There is a Son of David ruling over David's kingdom: Jesus Christ, the Son of God. (In human terms Jesus was of the line of David—see the genealogy in Matt. 1:2-16.)

But Jesus' kingship is far different from the rule envisioned by David. This was part of the problem Jesus had with His own people. They looked for a Messiah to be an earthly ruler. Jesus came as Messiah, but to be a heavenly ruler. They wanted a temporal king to overthrow the power of Rome. Jesus is an eternal king to destroy the power of evil. They looked for a material kingdom. Jesus rules over a spiritual kingdom. This is the meaning of Colossians 1:13-14.

Once again God has demonstrated His ability to go far beyond His promises as human beings understand them. In mathematics we talk about raising numbers to the "nth degree." This means an extremely large figure, usually more than can be determined by ordinary arithmetic. God "is able to do immeasurably more than all we ask or imagine" (Eph. 3:20).

GOD'S COVENANT WITH YOU

Will you look at yourself as a member of the covenant people of God?

You are a child of Abraham, "the father of the faithful." How does your faith "stack up" with his? Are you willing to exercise faith in God, hoping "against all hope" (Rom. 4:18), as he did? Remember that he did not always trust perfectly. But his focus was on God "who is able." Will you seek to trust God in the same fashion?

Now think of yourself as a member of God's chosen people, the church of Jesus Christ. What is your attitude toward others in this fellowship? Do you strive to have right dealings with them as evidence of your right relationship with God? Our obedience to God is shown by keeping His commandments, and these are fulfilled through love for one another. (See John 14:21; 15:9-12; 1 John 3:21-24.) Our love for God is shown by our love for all people, beginning with the other members of God's family, the church. How can you show yourself to be part of God's kingdom of priests and holy nation? Are you willing to be a "priest" to those who do not know Jesus

Christ? Will you witness to them daily through actions and words as you have opportunity?

This leads us to the fact that we are part of God's kingdom. As we saw earlier, we are partners with God now in bringing His kingdom on earth. This kingdom will never fail. Jesus said, "Do not be afraid, little flock, for your Father has been pleased to give you the kingdom" (Luke 12:32). This kingdom is our inheritance: "the kingdom prepared for you since the creation of the world" (Matt. 25:34).

NOTE

1. Handley Moule, "The Epistle of St. Paul to the Romans," *The Expositor's Bible,* ed. W. Robertson Nicoll (Grand Rapids, MI: William B. Eerdmans Publishing Co., 1940), p. 584.

8.

God Is Faithful in His Forgiveness

God is faithful in His forgiveness. In 1 John 1:9 we read, "If we confess our sins, he is faithful and just and will forgive us our sins and purify us from all unrighteousness." This verse and many others like it in the Bible should be of the utmost comfort to Christians. But strangely, they all too often do not take such verses to heart.

Christians are often painfully aware of their sins, even since they were redeemed. Most public prayers (and probably most private ones) include the phrase, "Forgive us our many sins," or, "Forgive us wherein we have failed Thee." But such prayers do not seem to reflect much assurance of forgiveness. Over and over the formula must be repeated. It does not seem that most Christians feel really sure of God's forgiveness of present sins. We can be assured that our former sins, which would have consigned us to hell, are forgiven and wiped out. But the burden of temptation, failure, and imperfection seems to lie heavy on the spirits of many Christians.

Accepting forgiveness is especially hard for persons who, like most Americans, measure acceptance by accomplishment. If persons have goals—in business, in school, in family relationships—they expect to reach those goals. If they do not, they are often harder on themselves than others may be on them. They beat themselves over the head for not being smart enough, energetic enough, persistent enough, lucky enough, or ruthless enough. Such persons do not forgive their shortcomings easily. So they find it difficult to believe in and accept God's forgiveness of their failings in His sight. Many persons come to Christian counselors with this complaint, that they cannot believe God would forgive them for their failures to live totally according to His will as Christians.

We also find it tough to forgive others. Often those who are closest to us are the hardest to forgive. We feel that they "ought" to know better. They ought to anticipate our needs and feelings; they ought to read our minds and hearts and act accordingly. Our sense of betrayal is therefore deeper, and it is that much harder to forgive these failings.

Some persons take sin and forgiveness too lightly. They are quick to express regret for their sins—to God or to their fellows—but this regret does not seem to be accompanied by a real desire to act differently. It is as if the very act of saying "I'm sorry" is all that is necessary. They do not examine the causes of their lapses, so it is easy for them to get into the same mudhole again. They then seem surprised, regretful, ask for forgiveness—and start the cycle all over again. Forgiveness should be given, but it should be accompanied by attempts to help such persons understand how and why their actions cause so much pain to others.

Jesus spoke forcefully of the need for forgiveness—both to give it and to receive it. He made willingness to forgive a condition upon which we receive forgiveness from God (read Matt. 6:12; compare Matt. 18:21-35). These words have caused considerable pain and confusion to conscientious Christians. They wonder how forgiveness can be conditional when it is offered so freely in many other biblical statements. To deal with these problems, we must understand forgiveness from God's perspective.

God's Forgiveness
Luke 15:23-32

Perhaps the best illustration of God's forgiveness is Jesus' parable of the prodigal son. We often study it from the viewpoint of the son's sin and restoration. We use it—rightly—to show how lost persons can be saved. But it is also a powerful parable of God's forgiveness and the need for persons to be forgiving, of themselves and of others.

We cannot understand this parable totally without knowing something of the laws of inheritance in Jewish life. The firstborn son received a double portion of his father's estate. Thus, if there were three sons, the estate was divided into fourths. The oldest son received two fourths or one half. The other two sons received one fourth each. Also, the estate was to be divided only upon the death of the father.

Look at the whole parable before studying it in detail. Note that the younger son would not wait until his father's death in order to receive his inheritance. His deepest sin was not the squandering of his father's possessions. His sin was the contempt and selfishness he showed toward his father. He demanded his share of the estate during his father's lifetime. It was as if he were saying, "Old man, I can't wait till you die. I want to live now. So give me what's mine."

Of course, the father's property did not yet belong to his sons. The father had full control of it. He did not need to give in to his younger son's arrogant demands. However, his love for his son was so great that he was willing for the young man to have his freedom from home, even at personal cost to himself. For the father gave up all his property—not only the part belonging to the younger son but the part belonging to the elder. The father was left nothing to call his own. He continued to live in a house and to farm property that no longer belonged to him.

Perhaps he also had to assume some losses. Maybe he had to liquidate some of his assets in order to pay his younger son in money. At any rate, the estate would naturally be somewhat impoverished by having to be divided prematurely.

None of this mattered at all to the younger son. He had what he wanted: freedom from his father, freedom from family obligations, and freedom from work for daily food. He seized all his possessions and set off for a distant country.

The inevitable happened, of course. The younger son had no idea of what it required to live. He used up his share of his father's property in a short time. He fell into poverty and near starvation. Then he came to his senses and began to long for home.

Notice his change of attitude. No longer was he arrogant and uncaring about his father. He recognized his sin in breaking the relationship. He cried out that he was no longer worthy of the father-son relationship. But he was destitute. He knew nowhere else to go. His pride was flattened, so he was willing to accept the place of a hired servant, working for board and keep on his father's estate. So he prepared a speech for his father and set out for home. Probably he rehearsed these words over and over, ready to speak them as soon as he met his father.

But his father acted in a manner that the son did not expect. He saw his son when he was "still a long way off" (v. 20). He was "filled with compassion for him." This word *compassion* means to be stirred in the depths of one's being by pity, sympathy, and concern. In the Gospels it is always used to express Jesus' deep concern for helpless and suffering people (see Matt. 9:36, 14:14; Mark 1:41, 8:1-2; Luke 7:13). So the father rushed out to meet his son on the road, threw his arms around the young man, and kissed him. His love and concern for this wanderer had obviously not diminished through the long period of absence.

In view of this expression of love, imagine what the father must have suffered while his son was in the "distant country" (v. 13). He must have wondered whether his son was dead or alive. He must have looked down that dusty road many times a day, hoping to see his son trudging along it.

Yet his son was "dead" to him, so far as their relationship went (v. 24). The son had cut himself off from the father, and there was nothing the father could do to change the situation. This, also, was part of the father's suffering. Love, when its object is removed, suffers.

But the father's compassion and love did not keep him from allowing his son's confession of guilt. He knew how necessary this was.

Imagine what would have happened if the son had come home with a different attitude . Suppose he had greeted his father with flippant words: "Hey, Dad! Here's that bad penny of yours turned up again! How about room and board for your baby boy? I've spent all you gave me. God anything put by that I can borrow?" Such words would have indicated that the son had learned nothing from his exile. He still would have been selfish, uncaring, contemptuous of the relationship. His confession of guilt cleared a path for a reestablishment of the father-son bond.

A most important ingredient of this story is the son's genuine repentance and his father's willingness to let him express it. The father did not interrupt him until the boy came to the place of asking to be treated like a servant. But the father let the son state his own recognition that he had broken the relationship.

This confession completed the father's joy in his son's return. The son was a different person from the self-willed ingrate who had left home. He had left without appreciation of his home. He returned willing to do anything to earn even a lowly place in his father's house. He had left denigrating his relationship with his father. He returned in full recognition of its value and conscious of what he had lost. He had left home with his hands full of his possessions. He returned with nothing—not even his pride.

No wonder his father could exclaim, "This son of mine was dead and is alive again" (v. 24). The son who had left home had been son in name only. Now he returned ready to be a son in love, obedience, and respect. This was truly like a new birth, and it was a cause for celebration.

Notice how full and immediate was the father's forgiveness. He did not make the son go through a probation period. He did not make him grovel in the dust or force him to pay back what he had wasted. The father restored him to full sonship, putting on him the attire appropriate to his status and calling for a gala feast.

This is true forgiveness! It wipes out the past and makes possible a glorious future.

But the story does not end there. Often those who tell the story stop with the celebration. In so doing they forget an important character: the older brother.

Coming in from the fields, he heard the sounds of a party. He asked a servant what was going on. When he heard that the celebration was in honor of his brother's safe return, he became furious. He refused to join the party.

His father went out to plead with him but could not persuade him. The son poured out his bitterness and anger to his father.

The words of this speech are revealing. Remember, he had received his share of the estate when his brother did, and his was the double portion. So what was left of the home property belonged to him. Yet his attitude toward his father was one of virtual slavery. He spoke of "slaving" for his father and never disobeying his orders (v. 28). He complained that his father had not so much as given him a "young goat" (of much less value than the fatted calf) so that he might entertain his friends. He seemed not to recognize that these animals were his to dispose of.

He had lived at home, but his relationship with his father seemed as far removed as his wandering brother's was. Furthermore, he had disowned his relationship with his brother. He snarled to his father, "This son of yours" (v. 30). He had cut himself off from his brother and did not know how to relate to his father.

The father gave him a gentle rebuke. "My son," he explained, "you are always with me, and everything I have is yours" (v. 31). He reminded the son of the realities of the situation. The son was not a slave but the owner of the estate. Their relationship should have been one of intimacy and warmth because they were always together. Celebration was called for when the lost was found, and the "dead" came "alive."

But the older son's unwillingness to forgive cut him off from the family. The story concludes with his still being outside the house and refusing to join the party.

This parable teaches us several vital truths about God's forgiveness. First is His willingness to forgive. His desire is for His wandering creatures to return to Him, to become genuine children in spirit. Second is the cost of forgiveness. No one—even God—who stands and waits for the return of the prodigal can escape suffering. Love thwarted in its desire ushers in suffering. This is the consciousness of what is missing in the relationship. It is also creative suffering because it seeks to do whatever can be done to win the loved one. Third is the quality of forgiveness. This is the kind of forgiveness that makes possible a new beginning and showers gifts of love upon the one who is forgiven.

One major question remains: If God is so ready to forgive, why does the Bible talk so much about His wrath? Can He not just forgive everyone their sins, so they will go to heaven? Some of this question has been answered in the chapter on God's holiness, yet it is appropriate to consider it here also.

God's Wrath
Ephesians 2:3; Romans 2:5-8; John 3:36

Ephesians 2:3 says that all humans "were by nature objects of wrath." Why is this so? Because of human beings' initial and continuing rebellion against God. This is the history of the human race. God's wrath comes because of humanity's rebellion. God does not "work up"

His wrath against His creatures. The wrath exists because of the nature of these creatures.

Human beings call down wrath upon themselves. Persons convicted of crimes need not be surprised to find the "wrath" of the law directed against them. The judgment of the law is there all the time. The person who breaks the law triggers the judgment of the law.

So Romans 2:5-8 contrasts the actions of those who trust God and obey His will with the actions of those who persist in rebellion. Notice that repentance and faith are necessary in order to please God. It is not the "doing good" (v. 7) that grants us eternal life. Such actions are the result of faith in God and proceed through His grace (see Eph. 2:8-10). The sin that triggers the wrath of God is unbelief. This is the meaning of John 3:36. God's wrath is always present toward rebellious humanity. It is removed when persons turn to Him in repentance and in trust of His Son as Savior.

GOD'S FORGIVENESS AND YOU

How does this analysis of God's forgiveness fit into your everyday living? Why is it so important to forgive others if our sins are freely forgiven by God?

The answer to this last question runs throughout the New Testament. But one major statement is found in Matthew 5:43-45. We are to cultivate a spirit of forgiveness, so we will be seen as belonging to the Heavenly Father. We are partners with Him in Kingdom building. The Kingdom advances as more people repent of sin and turn to God for forgiveness. If we are not forgiving—of ourselves and of others—the truth of God's forgiveness becomes blurred. How can we proclaim God's forgiveness unless we forgive?

Forgiving ourselves is often hardest to do. We do not

want to acknowledge our sins—to ourselves, to others, or to God. So the door to forgiveness is closed to us, or else, we see our sins so vividly that we stop loving our sinful selves. Such an unforgiving spirit spills over to others. A pungent observation is: "We condemn in others the sins we most despise in ourselves." Think about that, and consider how vehemently you condemn those who commit sins that you have—or might have—committed.

A forgiving spirit means doing good for those who are our enemies. Love toward all others, including enemies, means seeking their highest welfare. Paul stated clearly in Romans 12:17-21 how we are to treat enemies. We act toward them as God would—with love, consideration for their good, and a readiness to forgive. Of course, forgiveness is a two-way street. In a sense, we cannot truly forgive until the offending person accepts our forgiveness. Even God cannot do that. Our forgiving attitude, however, will be calculated to draw those offenders to us, so forgiveness may be asked and granted. (Often it must be granted on both sides. Few of us are offended against without our having some responsibility for the situation.)

Further, it is vital to remember that forgiveness does not restore a former relationship as if nothing had happened. Even the prodigal's father admitted a difference: "This son of mine was dead and is alive again" (Luke 15:24). A seminary professor of mine noted, "When God forgives, he pulls the nails out of the board, but even God cannot do away with the nail holes. We have to live with the consequences of our sin." So it is with all relationships. We cannot rub away the nail holes left by our sin or by the hurtful things done between persons. We must tenderly pick up the relationship and try to work creatively with it. God has plenty of things He can do creatively with nail holes. We also need to look for similar opportunities to make new relationships where the old ones have been scarred.

All these actions affirm our relationship to our Father in heaven. Our willingness to forgive and to build new relationships on the basis of forgiveness will expand God's kingdom. It will mark us as true partners in that kingdom. Then we can enjoy God's forgiveness as we work with Him in leading others to the throne of mercy.

9.

God Is Faithful
in His Final Triumph

When the trumpet of the Lord shall sound, and time
    shall be no more,
And the morning breaks, eternal, bright, and fair;
When the saved of earth shall gather over on the other
    shore,
And the roll is called up yonder, I'll be there.

      —James M. Black

When you read these words or sing them, what do they
mean to you? Are you thrilled at the idea of the end of
time? Do you wish for it to happen soon? Or do you shy
away from this idea: the return of the Lord in our lifetime?

God's final triumph is sure—the entire Bible witnesses
to that truth. No Christian would deny this doctrine, but
what does it actually mean to our everyday lives? Does it
make a difference to you, when you wake up on Monday
or Saturday, that Jesus might return that day?

Preachers used to hang onto the negative aspect of this
question. They would preach "morality sermons," asking,

"Suppose Jesus were to come while you were doing _____, how would you feel? Would you want Him to find you doing that?" They failed to point out that what each of us is doing is no news to Jesus! He knows our every thought, word, and action now. I haven't heard sermons like this in a long time, but I always disliked the feelings of guilt they used to engender. Surely, there should be a positive note connected with Jesus' return and the final triumph of God!

We no longer hear many references to the end of the world in the context of avoiding certain actions. It seems that most people's attitudes toward this great coming event fall into two camps. One group totally ignores any idea of Jesus' coming again. They believe it, but it really makes little or no difference to them. On the other hand, another group directs toward Jesus' return and the end of the world an extreme curiosity. They pore over verses of the Bible, trying to find references to point out the exact time of Jesus' coming. They tie current events into their reckoning so they can come up with a time.

Neither of these attitudes is acceptable to Jesus. He made plain, in His latest discourses before His death, that the attitude most pleasing to Him was one of constant, vigilant faithfulness. His servants were to be constantly ready for his return by always doing His will. He warned against trying to predict the exact time of His coming. Read Mark 13:32-37.

But is this all we are to do? Should we look forward to His return with joy or with a certain amount of dread? How do we interpret events in our world—and in our own lives—in the light of God's final triumph?

God's final triumph will come to pass when three things happen: when His love is satisfied, when His holiness is shown to be justified, and when His plan for His creation comes to fruition. Various Scripture passages speak regarding these things. We will study each one as the New Testament reveals it.

God's Love Satisfied
1 Corinthians 15:22-26, 42-44; Philippians 3:20-21

God's original plan for His human creatures was that they should be made in His image. They were created to love and adore Him and to share fellowship with Him forever, but their rebellion cut them off from Him. In their sinful state they could not be allowed to live forever with Him (see Gen. 3:22-23). Physical and spiritual death was the result of sin (Rom. 5:12; 6:23).

Through the new birth, based on faith in Jesus Christ, Christians now have within them the "seed" of eternal life. But we still are joined to a body that is destined for death. The promise of God, as shown in our Scripture passages, is that this body will be transformed from a physical to a spiritual body in the resurrection.

We know that our physical bodies are limited and are subject to illness and death. No matter how many advances are made by medical science, death is still sure. My husband has an aunt who is still amazingly vigorous at 105. By the time this book is being read, she may be gone—unless our Lord comes in the meantime.

Why should we need a spiritual body? We need it not only because our bodies are subject to death, but because they are very limited. When astronauts rocket into outer space, they must carry their environment with them. They could not live a minute without "earthly" air to breathe and other means of sustaining human life. But in God's universe there are no such limitations. The spiritual bodies we have will not be limited by time or space. They will be free and everlasting!

How do we know this? Because our bodies will be like the resurrected body of our Lord Jesus (Phil. 3:21). We will have "glorious" bodies. In other words, our bodies will reflect the glory of God just as Christ's body does.

Once that has happened, Christ's earthly work will be finished. He will be ready to turn over His "stewardship" of the kingdom to God the Father (1 Cor. 15:24-26). Once the possibility of death for God's children is destroyed, then God's plan will be complete.

We do not know, of course, how this miracle will be accomplished. It is not humanly possible to describe or explain such a transformation. Yet, we know it will happen. We have a special gift from God that guarantees it. We have "the promised Holy Spirit, who is a deposit guaranteeing our inheritance" (Eph. 1:13-14). We have within us the Holy Spirit of God. He is the "seed" who will burst into full life at the proper time. He is like the "earnest money" put down to guarantee a sale of property. Because we belong to God, He belongs to us. And through His power we shall become like the Lord Jesus and dwell as spiritual beings with God throughout all space and all time—through eternity.

Thus God's love will be satisfied. He will be surrounded by myriads of redeemed human beings sharing fellowship with Him and adoring Him for His love and grace. (Notice Rev. 21:3.)

God's Holiness Justified
Matthew 13:24-30,40-43; 25:31-46; John 5:28-29; 1 Corinthians 3:11-14; Revelation 20:11-15

Space will not permit extensive study of all these passages. But each of them contains important truths about how God's holiness will be justified by His final judgment of human beings.

Often we hear persons complain about the seeming injustice of God's dealings with human beings in this world. They see bad things happening to "good people" and, conversely, bad persons prospering. Then they ask, "Why?" It seems that if God is just, He should not let people get away with breaking His laws and refusing to accept His authority.

Jesus gave the best answer to this question in His parable of the wheat and the tares (Matt. 13:24-30,40-43). The weed seeds sowed among the wheat in the field may well have been "bearded darnel." This weed looks much like wheat as it forms heads, and often it cannot be distinguished from the wheat until the grains are fully ripe. So the owner of the wheat field (Matt. 13:29-30) ordered his servants to let all the plants grow together until harvesttime. Then the good grain could be gathered into the barn, while the weeds would be cut down and burned up.

So it is with good and evil persons in this world, Jesus taught (Matt. 13:37-43). It is not always possible to distinguish evil from good. What chaos might result if God were to destroy evil persons in the midst of history! In fact, we might be surprised at some of the persons whom God would consider evil. Families would be disrupted, governments might be torn up, ad infinitum.

God knows that this world is not the end of His plan or the final place of His reign. He lets good and evil live together until His time has come. Also, this is presently the time of God's mercy. So long as persons have life on this earth, there is the possibility of their repenting and being saved. Immediate justice and retribution on God's part would take away their chance (2 Pet. 3:8-9).

There is another point to be considered. Only at the end of history will the final effects of humanity's good and evil deeds be seen. So God's judgment will not be premature. Mordecai Ham, under whose preaching Billy Graham was converted, probably never preached in his whole lifetime to as many persons as Graham had in his early crusades of the 1940s and early 1950s. Yet his faithfulness in preaching will not be forgotten. I heard a preacher remark that if Ham had won only one person to Christ— Billy Graham—his life would have been well worthwhile. The same truth holds on the side of evil. Who can finally judge the effects of a life like Hitler's until the end of the ages?

So God's holiness will be justified as He rewards those who do good—truly trust Him—and banishes those who do evil—reject Him! But it will not be deeds that save or damn human beings. Their deeds will be the result of their natures.

In Jesus' parable of the sheep and the goats (Matt. 25:-31-46), He compared persons to animals familiar to His hearers. Sheep and goats had their characteristic patterns of acting. Their actions did not make them what they were; what they were determined their actions. So the children of God acted as those who were related to God. This is why they were so unconscious of their good deeds. They just did "what came naturally," according to the new nature! The same was true of the unrighteous persons, those who had no relation to God. They had acted according to their natures: self-concerned, uninterested in the plight of other human beings, unwilling to "put themselves out." Their sins were mostly those of omission. They refused to love their neighbors as themselves because they did not love God supremely.

Notice that righteous persons—those who are God's children—are also judged according to their deeds. Paul made this clear in 1 Corinthians 3:11-14. Often Christians seem to think that their lives on earth matter little so long as they are saved. But Paul emphasized that all we do has its part to play in God's building. The end of the world will be the time of purifying and destroying fire. Surely all of us would want to feel that our work for God will endure! It is not clear what kinds of good works might be considered "gold" and what kinds of actions might be considered "straw." A comparative study of Jesus' parable in Matthew 25:31-46 and this passage, along with our enlightened consciences, might help us to determine the kinds of actions that would endure in God's kingdom. Positive concern for fellow human beings would certainly be "golden."

All this judgment will come at the end of the age. Jesus pointed out that there will be two resurrections: "those who have done good will rise to live, and those who have done evil will rise to be condemned" (John 5:29). Most people who care nothing for spiritual life maintain that life on earth is all there is to existence. We die—and that's it. But that is not the witness of Scripture.

All persons are made in the image of God, and that image has been marred by sin. The relationship with God that His image was supposed to bring has been destroyed by rebellion. But the image evidently remains. At the resurrection of the dead, all those who have been born again will bear that image fully. Those who have never had a relationship with God will suffer spiritual death—the loss of the image of God within them. Revelation 20:11-15 speaks of this "second death."

But notice that such a fate is not God's will for human beings. This fiery death was "prepared for the devil and his angels" (Matt. 25:41). Those persons whose names are not "written in the book of life" (Rev. 20:15) have made their choice. By not choosing God and life, they have chosen the devil and spiritual death.

So God's holiness will be justified. His patience with the sins of humankind will be shown to be right. His mercy will be extended as far as possible to all persons, but his judgment on evil will be total and final. Everything and every person whose life and actions have worked against the righteousness of God will be banished from His presence.

When all these clouds of evil have been driven from the eternal sky, then the children of God will be clearly seen. "Then the righteous will shine like the sun in the kingdom of their Father," promised Jesus (Matt. 13:43).

God's Plan Completed
Romans 8:19-21; Revelation 21:1-4; 22:1-5

What more is necessary to make God's plan of the ages complete? The transformation of the natural created order is needed. God's universe is at bottom spiritual, but now it is seen in material terms. This is not the end of God's plan for His creation. We have already noted that spiritual bodies will be needed for human beings to exist in God's environment. So God will change the environment of the universe to provide a proper setting for His eternal children.

The passage in Romans 8:19-21 is full of mystery. Yet, its basic message is clear: God is not through with His universe. It will be recreated "from its bondage to decay." Now, the world we experience moves in cycles from life to death to creation of new life, from summer to fall to winter to spring and again to summer. All plant and animal life come into being in order to die. This will no longer be the case. The whole natural order will be "brought into the glorious freedom of the children of God" (v. 21).

But this cannot happen until the beings for whom the creation was made are ready for such a new environment. "The creation waits in eager expectation for the sons of God to be revealed" (v. 19). This "revealed" refers to the transformation of our bodies so that our true nature will be revealed as God intended it. When we are ready for a spiritual environment in which to live, God will provide it. We have no idea how this will be accomplished. It is not necessary for us to know. If we did, our finite minds certainly could not comprehend God's working. It is enough to have His faithful promise that this will come to pass.

We do have sort of a description of this new environment in Revelation 21:1-4; 22:1-5. I say "sort of" because this is John's attempt to describe spiritual wonders in material terms. No human being can presently comprehend the glories of the new universe. So John took the most beautiful physical objects he knew to describe spiritual wonders which he could discern with spiritual insight but could not describe in words.

"A new heaven and a new earth, for the first heaven and the first earth had passed away" (Rev. 21:1). This is the fulfillment of the prophecy in Romans 8:21. The "first" heaven and earth refer to the physical universe as we know it, subject to decay because it is of material substance. The new universe will be purely spiritual.

"No longer any sea"—this would be a particularly potent image to John in exile on the Isle of Patmos. The sea separated him from civilization, from friends, from his beloved church, from freedom to preach and to witness for Christ. No more sea stood for the absence of everything that would separate God's people from one another.

The center of this new universe is "the Holy City, the new Jerusalem" (v. 2). Jerusalem always stood for the dwelling place of God. In the new heaven and earth, there will be no limitations of time and space. All time will be swallowed up in eternity; all space will be swallowed by infinity.

So the real meaning of this picture is that God will be with human beings totally and forever. This is what God intended from the beginning. He walked with Adam and Eve in the Garden of Eden. His tent (or tabernacle) was carried with the people of Israel on their pilgrimage to the Promised Land. The Temple was the symbol af God's presence with His people. He was not confined to that building. But seeing it in their midst reminded the people of God's constant presence with them. Now symbol will become actuality.

God's presence will bring continual joy to His people. Death, mourning, crying, and pain are all results of sin in the world and in human lives. But after sin and death have been banished, not only from human lives but from the universe, there will be no need for mourning or crying.

The final picture of heavenly bliss shows how completely God's original plan will be carried out. Compare the description of the Garden of Eden (Gen. 2:8-10) with the description of God's dwelling place with humanity in Revelation 22:1-5.

Here we have the water of life and the tree of life. These figures are symbolic of the provision made for the eternal life of the redeemed. Further, the tree of life bears "leaves . . . for the healing of the nations" (v. 2). We are not sure exactly what this means. But we can be certain that it stands for a healthy state of affairs among all persons of whatever race, language, or social condition as they join together in the family of God.

"No longer will there be any curse" (v. 3). God cursed both humanity and His created order when human beings

rebelled against Him. Now that curse has been removed;
therefore, "his servants will serve him" (v. 3). Heaven will
not be a place of idleness but of service. Redeemed
humanity will be given opportunities of service to God in
His eternal kingdom of which we cannot even dream.
This service will be in the form of reigning over God's
kingdom forever (Rev. 22:5).

Most wonderful of all, we shall "see his face" (v. 4).
There will be no need for any kind of light, because God
will provide all the light needed in His creation by His
people. "There will be no more night" (v. 5). In the Bible
darkness always stands for sin, the power of evil, and lack
of ability to move about freely. No such hindrances will
exist in God's new heaven and earth.

Every blessing God has promised since the beginning of
human history will have been brought to pass when
God's plan is complete. We are assured this will happen
because we serve a God who is totally faithful. In Revelation 21:6 He says, "I am the Alpha and the Omega [as we
might say, from A to Z], the Beginning and the End." God
has not changed His mind, His character, or His promises
from all eternity. As we saw in the beginning of this book,
God makes His promises on the basis of who He is. So
nothing can or will divert Him from His purpose until His
every promise has been fulfilled.

YOUR PART IN GOD'S FINAL TRIUMPH

Yes, this is all wonderful, but what does it mean for us
where we are? We seem far removed from the glories of
heaven. We have to struggle with pain, temptation, suffering, death, injustice, and the forces of evil. But the point
is this: we struggle as soldiers who may lose a few skir-
mishes but who know the war is already won! The master

strategy for winning that war has already been drawn up and approved. It is a matter of time, only, until the warfare will be ended.

So we are to live joyfully even amid pain. We are to live victoriously amid seeming defeat. We are to live at peace in a world of raging war.

Further, in one sense, we are already living in heaven. We carry within us the power of eternal life. We know that "our citizenship is in heaven" (Phil. 3:20). Paul wrote these words to the Philippians. They clearly understood his meaning. Their city was a Roman colony. This meant that they had all the privileges that they would have if they lived in the city of Rome itself. Their dwelling place was many hundreds of miles from Rome, but they lived like Romans! So we—although heaven seems very remote —are to live by the laws and with the privileges of heaven. This is one of the constant themes of Paul's letters. (Read 2 Cor. 4:16 to 5:10.) "We live by faith, not by sight," he wrote (2 Cor. 5:7). So eternal values should continually become more important to us than earthly concerns.

Last, our heavenly life will be enhanced if we strive each day to live closer to the Lord Jesus, to God the Father, and to the Holy Spirit. I once read that one reason why unbelievers could not go to heaven was—they would be so uncomfortable there! Imagine persons who had made themselves the center of their lives, and had lived only for material gains, being thrown into the everlasting presence of a holy God. How miserable they would be! It would be like suddenly thrusting beings who had lived all their lives in dark, cold caves into the full light of the noonday sun. They could not stand such exposure!

All of us carry a few cold, dark places that cannot stand the light of God's sun. This is part of the old nature which continues to be part of our beings, but our lives will be enriched as we systematically expose our dark places to the glory of God's light. Each day should present new challenges to be more like Jesus. Each day should elicit new resolves to follow God's will. Each night should be a time of confession of shortcomings and sin and joy in the opportunities that may come tomorrow. Those who will be happiest in heaven will be those who have seen the "glory of God in the face of Christ" (2 Cor. 4:6). This should be our goal.

God will work with us in and through our struggles.

His divine power has given us everything we need for life and godliness through our knowledge of him who called us by his own glory and goodness. Through these he has given us his very great and precious promises, so that through them you may participate in the divine nature and escape the corruption in the world caused by evil desires (2 Peter 1:3-4).

Amen!